To Helen,
Best Wishes,
Jerome Art

Also by Jerome Arthur

Down the Foggy Ruins of Time
Life Could be a Dream, Sweetheart
One and Two Halves
The Muttering Retreats
The Journeyman and the Apprentice
The Death of Soc Smith
The Finale of Seem
Oh, Hard Tuesday
Got no Secrets to Conceal
Brushes with Fame

Antoine Farot and Swede

A Novel

Jerome Arthur

Antoine Farot and Swede

Revised Second Edition 2019
Published by Jerome Arthur
P.O. Box 818
Santa Cruz, California 95061
831-425-8818
www.JeromeArthurNovelist.com
Jerome@JeromeArthurNovelist.com

Dedicated to my Father

Acknowledgments

I wish to acknowledge the invaluable editorial assistance of Austin Comstock and Morton Marcus. Also, thanks to John Ton for the cover art.

One

Its colder'n a well diggers ass in the Klondike. Me and Swede hopped this freight car about an hour ago in Minneapolis. We think its goin to Milwaukee. At least we hope it is. With any kinda luck, we could be in New Orleans by the end a next week. I told Swede that since we was gonna be hungry and homeless, we didnt have to be cold, too. So that's when we both figured on goin south, which is where we're headin now. Yesterday afternoon at the Thanksgiving dinner table, I took a Louisville Slugger to that Polack son of a bitch my mother married about two years after she packed us up and moved away from Pop, which was when he walked out the door on his way to a pool game in some joint down on Lyndale Avenue. I remember how good a player he was. I guess I inherited it from im. I'm a pretty good shot myself. Once I peeked thru the window a some joint, and it was at that exact moment that he was runnin the table in a game a straight pool. God he was swell!

He was off to a pool game the day Ma left im. He was leavin the house, and she told im that her, my sister and me wouldnt be there when he got home, but I guess he didnt believe her cuz he went to the pool hall anyway. I cant hardly remember the event; its only the shadow of a memory from my childhood now, kept there by my sister who repeated the story over and over again. This was actually one a the more colorful stories she told about Pop, not one designed to make me feel guilty, which, I think, was her purpose most a the time when she talked about im to me. But when she told this story, a flicker a pride crossed her face as she described his swagger, sayin it made im appear a lot bigger'n he actually was. She said he looked dashing with his der-by hat cocked to one side, struttin down the alley that last time, disappearin around the corner as soon as he reached the street. At that same time Sis says Ma was tellin her to start gettin our stuff together. We was movin to a different place and wouldnt be seein too much of pop anymore.

Two years later, my mother met and married this little Polish tight wad. I guess she had a thing for little guys, but size was the only thing that fuckin ass-hole had in common with my father. Pop was a happy-go-lucky kinda guy that could talk to anybody. Just get a couple belts in im, and he was right at home in any company. If he had a couple bucks, he'd lose em or give em away in a minute. That was another reason why my mother left im. She thought he should take care of his family first. She was right. He used to al-ways bring me and my sister little presents and things, and he was always kind to my mother, but he was real irresponsible. He was probly the last person in the world to ever have a wife and kids and responsibilities, but somehow he was dealt that hand, and I guess you could say in the end he had to fold.

So, my mother married this hard-ass little Po-lack, that's so goddamn tight he squeaks. And he's got

8

this little-man complex, so he's always kinda belliger-ent. He's toughest on me, and then my ma. He never lays a hand on my sis. He dont physically beat my ma neither; its more a mental thing. But he's always got an excuse to hit me and beat me up. I guess he thinks it aint right to hit women, but men are okay, no matter how young or old they are. Well, somethin happened as the years passed. I started gettin bigger and stronger and I was learnin how to fight back. We're both about the same size now, but I'm gettin to be a better fighter than him. I guess I really didnt need to use the baseball bat. I'm already strong enough and big enough and wiry enough to go to fist city with im and take im, too, but I just got so goddamn pissed off at the little asshole that I went nuts, just for a minute, and put im down for the count with the bat.

The scariest part is I dont know if I killed the son of a bitch or not. Not scary cuz I might be guilty of murder or manslaughter, but scary cuz it would break my ma's heart if I did, and scary just the thought of killin another person. I mean, I killed plenty a squirrels with a slingshot before, but I dont know about killin a man. That's different. All I could think of was how tired I was of him beatin on us all the damn time. His relationship with my sister Megan seemed kinda twist-ed to me. He always treated her like I think he shoulda been treatin my ma. I dont know for sure, but I dont think theres anything queer goin on between em. Well, if there is and I killed im, there wont be from now on.

Last night in the jungle down near the train yard, we met James, and he took a likin to us right away and told us about this train goin to Milwaukee.

9

He told us to stick with him and he'd show us how to hop onto a movin boxcar. We joined im at a campfire with two other fellas. None of us had much for food. When I ran outa the house leavin Megan and Ma cryin over that old cheap skate, I grabbed a bag a the doughnuts Ma makes every day. She makes em and I roam the streets sellin em. Well, I grabbed a bag before I ran outa the house, and Swede managed to get a hold of a half a loaf a bread when he left his house. One a the other men had stolen a can a Campbells tomato soup he heated in an old coffee can over the open campfire. With the soup and doughnuts and bread, the five of us managed to have a pretty good meal. After we ate, James played his mouth organ, and its strains were ever so comforting in a forlorn and melancholy way. Right now, I'm kinda sad and lonely and I'm not alone. By no later than nine oclock we was huddled together in the cold Minneapolis night, sleepin around the well-stoked campfire. It was freezin cold, and I was glad we was gonna be headin south, and for the first time in my life, I was gonna be someplace in the winter and there wouldnt be snow on the ground.

A few minutes before dawn James was stirrin the hot coals of the fire and throwin the last pieces of wood on so we could have a fire to warm up some water for coffee when the sun came up. He said a Chicago bound freight would be leavin at nine oclock. We wanted to be on it, but we had to keep a keen eye out to make sure we didnt get pinched by the railroad dicks that are always tryin a throw guys off the trains. By the time the sun broke over the horizon, all of us that slept by our campfire were awake and gatherin our stuff to-gether.

There was still four doughnuts left in the bag. Before I left the house, I took the wool army blanket off my bed and rolled an extra pair a trousers and a shirt up in it and tied it with an old piece a clothesline. This was my travelin baggage. I split two of the doughnuts five ways and rolled the other two in their bag into the bedroll with my other things. I gave one piece each to Swede, James and the other two fellas at our campfire, and had the last piece for myself. We ate em with hot coffee in old tin soup cans, which also warmed our hands on this freezin November mornin. Good thing the sun came out. Its actually turned out to be a fairly warm day. It was full above the eastern horizon by eight oclock, and by nine oclock we was hoppin this freight headin for Chicago. Probly stop in Milwaukee first.

The last sign I seen on a station was Winona. So far we been lucky not to get rousted by bulls. The most uncomfortable part has been the freezin cold in this boxcar. Everybody in here's afraid to build a fire cuz the smoke will only bring the bulls down on us. Me and Swede are wrapped up in our blankets and we've got James in between us. Its better'n nothin, but its still cold. Good thing James is with us cuz some a these other fellas look like theyd try takin our blankets if all they had to deal with to get em was a couple teenage boys. They see James with us and they keep their distance.

I guess we'll be stickin with James for quite a while. He's goin where we're goin, and for the same

11

reason; he wants to get warm, too, plus he wants to find his ex-wife, and she's out on the west coast. He was married and him and his wife were pretty well off until the crash when he lost his job and couldnt keep her in the style she was used to, so she left im and ran off to Hollywood with some big shot producer. He said she got a couple roles in B movies that didnt go nowhere in the theaters, but the last he heard, she was still out there and doin' pretty good. He even has it half way in his head that he's gonna go all the way out there and look her up. If he does, I guess we'll be stickin with im all the way. Our goal is to get to a place called Seal Beach, which is someplace out in Southern California; I'm still not sure where. Swede knows. He's got an aunt livin there. If she'll have us, we plan to stay with her until we get jobs and then we'll get our own place. James says when we get to Milwaukee, we're probly gonna have to get off before we get to town and walk ahead and catch it at the other end goin out. The word is that this train's gonna lay over in Milwaukee for a couple hours. That should give us time to make it to the other end and catch it to Chicago.

Looks like we'll be ridin these rails for who knows how long, not knowin whether the Polack is dead or whether I only put im on queer street for a while. Its probly not such a swell idea that it happened on Thanksgiving, but goddamn it, I was tired of the abuse. You can only go so long always gettin the fat and gristle, and we was dirt poor. I guess you could say we was asphalt and concrete poor since we was livin in the city. My stepdad aint worked since the stock market crashed two years ago. My ma makes swell dough-

12

nuts, so she'd make up ten dozen or so, and then I'd peddle em around town, gettin around by hoppin on the back a streetcars, gettin a dime a dozen. That was always worth a buck or so a day, which was more'n we was gettin from Wiktor. Megan took in washin and ironin and made a couple bucks a day that way. It was hard times, and we was lucky to be gettin that much.

So, the three of us are bustin our asses tryin to make some dough, and when we do and Ma buys some meat, the old man takes the lean and gives us the gristle. Well, Thanksgiving rolled around, and we got an early chill outa the north, and we had to get extra coal before the end a the month cuz it was so goddamn cold, and theres just generally bad times all around. We was even cuttin the milk with water so that it would go further. Ma got this small ham for Thanksgiving dinner, and there wasnt much lean on it. There was quite a bit a fat, but it was all we could afford. Wiktor takes and cuts the fat off the ham, and divides it up three ways for Ma, Megan and me. Then he takes all the lean pork and starts carving it for himself. Not that we didnt expect somethin like that to happen. He done it before. I ate it before (I poured syrup over it so it would at least taste sweet) cuz if I didnt, I wouldnt have anything to eat, and I'm a growin boy, and sometimes we'd go for a whole week without any meat a-tall. Doin it to us on Thanksgiving was the last straw. I had enough; I couldnt take no more, so I got up and went over and took his plate and set it in the middle a the table and started cuttin what was on it into four portions. He got up from his chair and cuffed me up side the head and started takin his plate back. That was when I got the

13

baseball bat and just clubbed that fuckin jerk as hard as I could. He went down to the floor and didnt move. It scared the shit outa me.

I went over to my chest a drawers in one corner a the room (it was basically a two-room bungalow with a kitchen), got some a my things out, wrapped em up in my army blanket, and hit the road. My first thought was to head south cuz I wanted to get warm. As cold as it is right now, I know its gonna be freezin, or even colder, soon. I went over to Swede's house. He's been my best pal ever since we was walkin home from school together one day, and four other fellas jumped us and the two of us kicked their asses. We was best friends after that, and we been constant pals ever since. He helped me sell the doughnuts. When we worked together, we got business up to twenty-five dozen doughnuts a day, and Sis helped Ma with the cookin.

So, havin my mind made up that I was leavin town, I walked over to Swede's to say goodbye or see if he wanted to come with me. He's been gettin the same shit at his house as I've been gettin at mine, but his comes from his real dad. I wonder if things woulda been any different if my Pop was livin with us instead a Wiktor. Times are tough. Theres a depression on. People're outa work, and that seems to make em irritable and in a bad mood all the time. Me and Swede aint the only ones neither; I know some other kids that're gettin beat up by their dads, too. Must be a sign a the times.

I went over to Swede's house with my bedroll tucked under my arm. I was wearin a pretty heavy, red

14

and black, plaid, wool jacket. Its probly the only good-quality thing I got to my name. I kept my head warm with a brown checked, eight panel, wool Donegal Newsboy.

Swede's family Thanksgiving ended in a fight, too. By the time I got there, he'd already left the house, and nobody knew where he was. I knew where to find im. I went over to the playground where we hung around on warm summer days, tryin to get the girls to go off in the bushes with us. He was there, by himself, sittin in the bleachers next to the ball diamond. I climbed up and sat down next to im and told im I was runnin away. I didnt even have to finish tellin im about it before he was on his feet and ready to go back to his house and get his stuff so we could get outa there together as quick as possible. It wasnt as easy for him to get away from his house as it was for me. My stepdad, if he was still alive, was probly glad to be rid a me, but I think Swede's dad wanted to keep im around so he could beat on im some more. He had to go back home, get his stuff, and sneak out without gettin caught.

He left me in the park and walked back home. It took im about an hour, but he finally came back. He was wearin a heavy, black, wool jacket, and a knitted, navy-blue watch cap. He had his things wrapped in a heavy wool blanket. We'd be glad real soon that we had those blankets. He pulled a letter outa the breast pocket of his jacket and showed it to me. It was actually an empty envelope with a canceled two-cent stamp on it. It was addressed to his mother, and the return address was Ingrid Johnson with a post office box in Seal Beach, California. He told me that Ingrid Johnson

15

was his aunt, his mother's sister, and we should try to get to her place. He said his aunt's always writin to his mother how warm and sunny it is where she lives. He stuffed the envelope back inside his coat, and we started walkin to the switichin yard over between Washington Avenue North and the river where Plymouth Avenue crosses and hung around a while tryin to figure out what to do. My idea was to try and get to Chicago. I figure its probly the train hub a the country, and most likely there'd be a lota traffic goin outa there, specially traffic headin south. If we could get to Texas, maybe we could get work on a ranch somewhere, or as rough necks in the oil fields. To me the most important thing is to get into the warm weather.

So, we was hangin around the switichin yard tryin to figure which train to hop to get to Chicago. I walked by there a lota times before and seen men gettin on and off the freight trains. They all seemed to hang around this one spot which was at the edge a the switichin yard where the trains were still goin slow enough for em to jump on. We was standin behind this group where a few stragglers walked up and down. It was startin to get dark, which is the best time to dodge the bulls that seem to appear from nowhere to roust bums and hobos travelin aimlessly thru this depression, lookin for work at every stop, lookin for somethin to eat when theyre too hungry to go on. Me and Swede joined their ranks. Its scary as hell, but its also an adventure, and it aint no scarier than goin back to face murder or manslaughter charges, or worse yet, to face Wiktor Sadlo.

16

ANTOINE FAROT AND SWEDE

When we realized that it wasnt such a smart idea to travel at night cuz a the cold, we wandered over to one a the campfires, and that's when we met James. We hit it off with im right away, and he told us to stick with im and he'd show us which train was the one we wanted. The first thing we learned from im was that we wouldnt be goin straight to Chicago, but to Milwaukee first and then south to Chicago, where, he told us, we'd be able to catch a freight to just about any place in the country we wanted to go. He said the last steady job he had was in Kansas City in twenty-nine at the time a the Crash. Since bein on the bum, he picked up odd jobs here and there, which mostly just paid im with a free meal. As we sat around the fire with the other two bums, James pulled out his mouth organ and started playin some mournful music. The music and the train whistles gave me this lonesome, melancholy feelin, and the ragged men I seen scramblin up and down the rails lookin for trains to catch only made me more lonesome.

I dont think I ever felt that lonely before in my life. This was it. We was on our own. We was gonna have to fend for ourselves. No more mother to go home to for comfort in time a trouble. Course our mothers couldnt be much comfort to us anyway; theyre tryin to keep their husbands happy and dont have time for our problems. I love my mother, and I'm already beginnin to miss her. The terror in her scream and the look on her face when I left the house is already hauntin me. I wanna reach out to her, to reassure her that I'll be all right, and that this is gonna pass, too, but I cant do that.

17

Jerome Arthur

Now I'm a fugitive, like the wind, and I have no idea how far I'll have to run, or how long I'll be runnin.

Two

I guess Ma and Pop made a deal when it came to naming me and Sis. The idea was Ma would name the girls and Pop would name the boys. Minding his Canadian French ancestry, Pop named me Antoine. His name is André. Our last name is Farot. My ma, whose maiden name was Kathleen Sullivan, stuck with her Irish ancestry, and named my sister Megan. Both Sis and me take a lotta ribbin about our last name. If it aint Farthead, its Fartface, or for her, the worst, Farthole. Megan always takes more shit than me, I think, cuz she's a girl, and cuz of the mixture of nationalities in her two names. Me, I dont take too much shit before I start kickin whoever's ass it is that gives it to me. Girls cant just up and kick someone's ass. I stick up for her whenever I'm with her and hear someone givin her a bad time, but I aint always there.

My dads people came from Quebec by way a Buffalo, New York and my ma's came from Ireland thru Boston. Its a strange mixture, and I'll be damned if I ever heard how they got together, but they was together until I was eight years old. Megan was ten. I cant ever remember my pop havin any kinda steady job, but yuh know, he could speak French just like he grew up in Paris or Quebec, and besides bein a swell pool player, he knew a lot about a lota things. I remember once hearin im tell one a his friends how a car works, and he never even had a car. He told this pal a his all about the internal combustion engine, how the spark plugs fired the pistons, which turned the crankshaft. The transmission connected the power to the rear end, which then turned the wheels and made the car go. The way he explained it was so clear. I didnt know he knew so much, and I knew then just as I know now that he could do the same thing with a whole bunch a other subjects. Just a little while ago, after I told James some a these things about my pop, he gave me the word for what Pop is: renaissance man. I like the sound a that.

After we moved out on Pop, I'd see im sometimes down on Hennipen Avenue, one a the streets where I had good luck sellin doughnuts, and we'd talk for a little while, and then he'd give me some a the coins he always seemed to have in his pocket, and head straight into some joint to hustle a game a pool. I'd sneak in and watch im beat one guy after another. I think the only money he ever had was his winnings from those pool games. I never knew where he was livin then. I knew he didnt live in our old house cuz when I went by there, I seen a whole other family there. I'd see im like that until I was almost thirteen, and then I didnt see im no more. Its been almost two years since the last time I seen im. I dont know what ever happened to im. He just quit showin up down on Hennipen Avenue, and I didnt know where else to look for im. By that time Ma was already with Wiktor Sadlo (he shortened his name from Sadlowski) for three years. They got married when I was ten and Megan was twelve. I dont think Megan ever saw Pop after we moved out on im. She didnt like im for some reason. I felt bad for Pop's sake after Ma married the Polack, - cuz Megan got along real good with *him*.

We crossed a river and it looks like theres a town up ahead. We all get a little on edge when we get close to a town, keepin our eyes open for bulls. The train slows a little bit as we come to the town. I get up close to the openin in the door and as we rock and roll on thru, I see the words La Crosse painted on a wooden cross sign next to the rail bed. If the sign wasnt painted on it, the cross looks like it could be on a church steeple somewhere. This freight aint losin no time, which is real keen. Long as we're movin this fast, the bulls cant roust us out, and before we know it, we'll be in Milwaukee. Its still real cold, but we're keepin warm by huddlin together. I guess we're movin south and east, but it sure aint gettin no warmer yet. I think that's why we aint seein no head knockers. The bulls around here must be fair weather head knockers.

The best luck we had was meetin up with James. He aint told us how old he is, but I'm thinkin he's about thirty-five, and that's only a guess. I aint real clear on what it was he was so successful at before the stock market crashed, but he said it gave im a pretty good life. He said he had a nice house with carpets and drapes and indoor plumbing and electricity. He says he wore evenin dress a lot, and his wife was a real knock-out in her satiny full-length evenin gowns. They was all caught up in the excitement that was goin on in the twenties. Nightclubs and speakeasies, dancin and drinkin. Him and his wife were just havin a good old time. He said he still loved her, and when he said it, he got this dreamy, far away look in his eye, and he quit

21

talkin, and, without bein real aware of it, he took his mouth organ outa the pocket of his tattered double-breasted wool suit coat and played one a those mournful tunes I'm startin to get used to. I think maybe I'd like to learn to play it myself. I wonder if he could teach me. I wonder if I could learn it. I dont feel like theres too much music in me. I know I couldnt carry a tune in a handcart, but maybe I could learn an instrument like the harmonica.

So, when the stock market crashed, James lost everything cludin his wife, and he says he woulda liked to hang around where he was, which was Kansas City, but he couldnt get any kinda steady work, and since his wife left, he had nothin but bad feelings for the place, so he decided to hit the road, and that's where he's been ever since. Says he stopped in a couple places that he's liked, but he keeps movin on again, supposedly to Hollywood where he's hopin he'll see his ex-wife. He aint made it there yet, but he says he's gonna make it this time. I hope he does cuz that means we'll make it, too. I think we'll make it anyway; me and Swede're tough. I guess you could say we're survivors. Now, we dont go out and look for fights on purpose, but I can honestly say that both of us can take care of ourselves, and together, we're real tough (I say impossible) to take. In fact, the further we go on this freight train with these other men, the more I think we could probly take real good care of ourselves if we didnt have James. Most a these fellas look real beat down. I dont think me and Swede have got that wore out yet, but who knows, we're only startin out.

ANTOINE FAROT AND SWEDE

Theres five other men in this boxcar, and only one of em looks like he could be any kinda trouble. I dont even know why I say that. Its only that he looks a little shifty to me, and he seems to be sneerin, where the other fellas look more tired than anything else. The three of us talked about it a little bit and they dont trust im neither, so we're gonna keep an eye on im. With any kinda luck, if we keep movin like we been movin, we wont be on any boxcar with im at night. Course in this cold weather we aint gonna be rollin at night anyway.

We keep movin along for a couple hours, and not much happens. The three of us stay huddled together. As the train slows down at the towns along the way, I get up and walk across the beat-up wood and steel floor to see their names: Tomah, Dells, Portage, and one that didnt have a sign along the tracks. We must be gettin pretty close to Milwaukee. The train is startin to slow down pretty quick all of a sudden. Everybody in the car starts movin around. You can sense somethin's goin on. Swede, James and me roll up our bedrolls and go over to have a look. The trains only goin about ten miles an hour. About a quarter mile up the track, we see comin toward us five big sturdy men with pistols strapped to their sides and carryin billy clubs. As they come up next to the engine, we scramble over to the other door and look out that side. Nothin in either direc-tion for as far as we can see. Next thing I know, we're all jumpin off the train.

Luckily, the weeds're tall here, and there aint a lota rocks and stuff. When I jump back up onto my feet, I see that James and Swede are both on their feet,

23

too, but Swede's hoppin around holdin onto his left hand. Looks like he hurt his wrist. He's jumpin around and holdin it and cussin up a storm. We scramble to get our bedrolls. When James and me come up to im, we see his wrist is swollen big as a grapefruit. I've had that happen to me before and I know it hurts like hell. Breakin it probly hurts less. Not far up the tracks the train comes to a stop. We run off into a small clump a trees right there and huddle in some underbrush. Tramps are scramblin all around us, but the bulls are stickin close to the tracks. It dont look like they caught anybody. They look more like theyre only flexin their muscles and not really serious about arrestin anybody or roughin anybody up. After theyve gone back to where they came from, we move back out into the open under the warm sun. We watch the train pull away up ahead. We find us a little spot in the sun and sit down, where we watch all the rousted hobos walk off in the direction of the retreatin freight train.

"Well, boys," James says, "we might as well pitch camp here for a little while. At least till your hand feels better, Swede."

"I think we should move on," Swede says. "We wont ever get south if we dont keep movin. Antoine here's gonna freeze up on us if we dont get im to some warm weather."

"He's got a point there," I say, "but I dont wanna move on if yer gonna be hurtin."

"Nothin to it," he says. "Its only my wrist. I can still walk, so I guess I'm lucky it aint my ankle."

We get goin right away. All the others that jumped off the train with us disappeared off up the

24

tracks ahead of us. I'll be damned if I know where those bulls came from or where they went to. Did they take our place on the train and ride on into Milwaukee? Probly not. That'd be too cold for em. They probly got into the caboose. Now we're stuck in the middle a nowhere, but you can kinda tell theres a town not too far up the track. Its slow goin, but with the cold weather, we walk a brisk pace to keep warm. I'm carryin both Swede's and my own bedroll. That way he can keep his lame hand in his jacket pocket.

After walkin for about an hour, we see a siding and water tank up ahead. When we get closer to it, we can see there aint nobody around. Its probly around one or two oclock by now, so we stop right there to have a lunch a doughnuts. We climb up on the platform and sit down. I take the bag with the two doughnuts outa my bedroll and break one up into thirds. As we sit there, we hear a train whistle comin outa the northwest. We gather up our stuff and move away from the track and into the bushes. The train rumbles around the last bend, and we watch it pull up to the siding and stop. As it sits there, another locomotive pullin a tender and a caboose whistles along from the opposite direction. The westbound locomotive stays on the main track steamin past the siding and disappearin into the northwest. When its gone, the eastbound train pulls up to the end a the siding to the water tank. Its got a whole bunch a flatcars and boxcars and one water tank car right behind the tender. We sneak out from the bushes at about the second car behind the water tank car and move down the track toward the end a the train. We find us a boxcar before we reach the caboose and we climb aboard. Shortly after we get on board, the wheels start turnin, the train lurches forward and we're on the rails again.

Three

That turned out to be a lucky ride. It took us all the way thru Milwaukee to a train yard at the south end a town. We finally turned the bend and we're headin south. It should be easy to catch a freight from here to Chicago, but its startin to get late so we're gonna have to camp here overnight and try to catch somethin in the mornin. Its kinda funny how this freight hoppin crowd is a world of its own. I'm startin to see people I seen in Minneapolis, and that shifty lookin bastard on that train we got rousted from is over there at a campfire with five other fellas. James seems to know quite a few fellas here. He's fixin it so we'll have a fire to sleep next to, and I think as soon as he gets us set up with one a these groups, maybe me and Swede'll go into town to see what we can dig up to eat. We still got one doughnut and a little bit a the bread left, but that's all we been eatin for the last day and a half, and I wanna get some nourishment in me.

We find a group a fellas that all seem to be pretty good guys, and we join em at their campfire. Swede's hand is still swole up, and its black and blue. He's been tryin hard not to move it around too much. Its gettin on to sunset, and we wanna get into town before it gets too dark, so we roll up our bedrolls and leave em with James, and we start on our way. When we come outa the switichin yard, we come into a kinda warehouse area. From there we go into a shabby tenement neighborhood with sleazy cafes where old men with rotten teeth and blank stares look into the void of half-empty coffee cups. Just as we come outa that neighborhood, passin a row of tenements, we see a well-dressed, well-off lookin man come down the stairs of one a the apartment houses and get into a waitin taxi cab. As he slides into the back seat a the cab, a piece a paper flutters away from his heavy topcoat just when we're passin. The taxi drives off into the Milwaukee dusk, and at our feet is a clean crisp five-dollar bill. What a stroke a luck that was.

We walk a little further and we're on the edge a downtown. For the first time since we left Minneapolis, we see men in soup lines. We walk right past em lookin for a grocery store. We pass a cross street, and theres one down the block. We head right for it. So far I noticed the best thing to do about food in these hobo camps is to get canned food, cuz if you dont open it, you can store it for quite a while. You dont wanna get stuff that's gonna rot on yuh. I get a can a Heinz baked beans, a can a Campbells soup and a quart bottle a milk. Swede buys a half dozen eggs for breakfast. That's one for every man at our campfire. We pick up a loaf a bread and some coffee and set our purchases down on the counter in front of a grocer that's lookin at us real suspicious. When Swede asks im for a half pound a bacon from the butchers counter next to the cash register, he demands to see some dough. When we produce the fin, the skeptical look disappears and he slices us up a half a pound a bacon and rings everything up on his cash register. The total comes to a buck fifty, and he gives us three-fifty for change. I have an

28

inside pocket with a zipper in the linin a my coat, and that's where I put the change.

We start back to the train yard with our goods. The streets are crowded, mostly men loiterin around or standin in line waitin for somethin to eat. A cop poundin his beat gives us a funny look, so we speed up our pace, but as we get outa his sight, I realize he was lookin at everybody real suspicious. Nighttime has fell. It is now dark as we retrace our steps back to the train yard and find our way to the campfire where we'll be spendin the night. When we show em what we got, they all get excited and start stirrin around the campfire, everybody doin' different jobs to get things ready for our baked beans and soup dinner. These other three fellas are bindle stiffs, each one with his own gunnysack filled with cookin gear. One of em has a saucepan, another has a fryin pan, and the third has a coffee pot and another sauce pan. They get out the coffee pot and the two sauce pans and start warmin things up. We all have a good meal, and theres nothin left over. I set the bacon and eggs as far away from the fire as I can to keep em cold until mornin when we'll cook em in the fryin pan.

As it gets darker, it gets colder. This is a different kinda cold than in Minneapolis. You can feel the wind comin off the lake, and cuz its so damp, it cuts right thru yuh. After we finish eatin, we sit around the campfire with our blankets over our heads and wrapped around our bodies. James is playin "Oh! Susanna" on his mouth organ, and one a the bindle stiffs, Johnny by name, the one that owns the coffee pot and sauce pan, joins im on banjo. As theyre playin, the shifty lookin

29

guy from the train earlier in the day walks past our campfire. He walks within two feet a the eggs and bacon and looks down at em and then at me as he passes. Arthur, the other bindle stiff, tells me he's seen im around quite a bit.

"Word has it, he carries a sharp knife. I aint never seen it myself, but I heard plenty about it. Goes by the name a Mousey, and you can understand why if you look at im close up," Arthur says. "I heard he knifed a bull over in North Platte, Nebraska. Some even say theres a price on his head over there. Yuh know I dont want no truck with no little weasel like him, but I can understand how a fella can get so desperate that sometimes he'll do somethin he maybe wouldnt do otherwise. If they dont do somethin about this money and job situation, we'll end up bein a country a nomads."

"Looks to me like we already are nothin but a bunch a drifters," I tell im, lookin all around me. "Take a look around, man. Everybodys on the move."

"I'll tell yuh, I'd sure like to settle in one spot," he says. "I'm gettin too old fer all this travelin. Gonna be forty-three on my next birthday, and all this movin, not to mention livin out in the weather, is startin to wear me down. Only trouble is, I wouldnt know where to go to settle down. Cant go back to Albany. I left a wife and three kids there. Dont think theyd wanna see me again. Just walked out on em after a year a not workin."

"Well, so far we been pretty lucky since we been on the road," I say. "Course, we only just started out yesterday."

ANTOINE FAROT AND SWEDE

"I was havin a good time when I started out, too, but its been what? A good year since then. And I wasnt even as young as you. I think I'm ready to quit."

James and Johnny are playin and the other bindle stiff, Leon, has joined em doin' vocals, singin union songs. The train whistles dont sound lonely tonight like they did last night. Except for missin Ma a little, I'm not homesick a-tall. Things around here are mournful and melancholy, but mostly the people I'm with are all good fellas. I feel better with them than I ever did with the old Polack. I look off to the next campfire and see Mousey lookin at me and at our breakfast. I wonder if he knows that he's got to deal with all six of us if he fucks around with the eggs and bacon. I'm the closest one to them and to him, so I guess I'll be the first one to have to go up against im, but it wouldnt be long before the other fellas would get into it. Swede alone, and with only one hand to boot, would kill im.

Swede says his wrist is givin im some pain, but it dont look like its got any worse. He's a tough son of a bitch, so I expect it wont slow im down none. Of the two of us, he's the big one. He's about five ten and weighs about a hundred and seventy. He's got reddish blond hair and blond eyebrows. Kinda yer typical Minnesota swede. I imagine we look quite the pair, him so big and blond, me so little and dark. My skin color is light, but I have black wavy hair that I comb straight back. Ma, Pop and Megan all have thick black hair, too. I'm only five seven and weigh a hundred and forty. I grew seven inches last summer right after my fifteenth birthday. I think I might be done growin. I'm small, but quick. I think itll be my quickness that's gonna save our bacon and eggs later on. Swede's quick, too, for a big guy, and he's next closest to the food. Fact is, he's a real good athlete. If he woulda stuck around and gone on in high school, he woulda made first string on the baseball team, I have no doubt. He's a swell first baseman, and he hits the hell outa the ball, but I guess that's all behind im now.

The hours pass and all the tramps start curlin up around their fires and goin to sleep. James, Johnny and Leon have stopped their playin and singin, and we're all starin into the fire not really havin a lot to talk about. The night is crisp and clear. Its gonna be cold in the mornin. I've moved the bacon and eggs in their bag so theyre right in between me and Swede. As the night moves on to the witchin hour, I fall asleep, and then sometime in the night I have a dream. I'm back home, and I'm on Nicollet Avenue right in the middle a downtown. Theres lots a people walkin the streets, and all the businesses are busy. It looks like the depression's over. Suddenly, Ma and Sis appear. It looks like theyre standin on the corner waitin for a streetcar. They turn my way, and when they recognize me, Ma tells me I've got to get away cuz theyre after me for what I done to Wiktor. Megan starts lookin for a cop; she wants to turn me in. I start to run and dont go nowhere; my heart's beatin like crazy; and that's when I wake up and I can tell its the coldest, darkest hour just before dawn. Theres frost everywhere, on the ground, on my blanket, and on everybody else's, too. My ears and nose are freezin. I just bundle up and snuggle up next to Swede and James and go back to sleep.

Four

We're in the southern tip of Illinois. We moved along pretty good since we left Milwaukee. We had some good luck and some bad luck. The good luck was goin almost all the way thru the state of Illinois without makin any stops. We hopped a southbound freight outa Chicago not fifteen min-utes after we jumped off the other one, and we didnt see any yard bulls for the short time we was there, probly cuz it was rainin. The bad luck came a couple hours ago when we got chased off the train in this heavy downpour. We're right in the middle of a flood, helpin a farmer move bales a hay into place to keep a creek from floodin his house and barn. I say its a creek. Right now, its a ragin river, and if we dont get these bales in place, the poor guy might lose everything. Swede's hand has got bet-ter, but he's still nowheres near a hundred percent. James cant do much with his bad arm. When we got rousted by those ridin bulls, he took a shot in the arm with a club that looked like a pick handle. He dont think he broke it; he thinks maybe it just got bruised real bad. Martha, the wife of the farmer that took us in, wrapped it up real good, and she thinks itll be okay if James takes it easy for a while. Four of us are movin bales to stop the flood: Oscar, his daughter Amelia, Swede and me.

If the rain would only stop, maybe some a this water would go down, and we could take a break, but it aint doin' that. Its comin down pretty hard. I guess we should be thankful cuz its warmed up since it started rainin. Its still plenty cold, tho. So far we're winnin the battle with the creek, but we wont be if the rain dont let up. Amelia's doin' a good job. She's a strong, wholesome seventeen-year-old farm girl. Her ma is tendin to James and helpin us some. We just about got all the bales right around here stacked. Theres some others off in the field that we'd have to use the horse and cart to get if we need em. Oscar was lucky they didnt sell in the hay market, cuz now theyre just laying out there waitin to be bought or be used as a levee. Its still rainin, but it seems to of let up a little bit.

So, what happened since Milwaukee? We made it thru the night and Mousey didnt try anything. In the mornin we fried our bacon and eggs in the skillet and had hot coffee and tried to toast some bread over the open fire. We didnt catch a freight car outa there till almost noon, but once we started to roll, it was a quick haul down to Chicago, only a couple hours. We got on a southbound freight outa Chicago by two-thirty, and we went all the way to Carbondale where the train made its first stop. We didnt know it at the time, but the only reason they stopped was to take on some bulls. It was rainin pretty good around Champaign, and by the time we hit Carbondale, it was comin down even harder. When the train got about a quarter mile from where we are right now, it stopped and the ridin bulls rousted us out into the rain and busted up James's arm in the bargain.

From where we got off the train, we could see this farmhouse and barn, and nearby was a gravel high road that brought us here. We was only lookin fer cover against the rain, maybe in the barn, but when we got here, we saw Oscar, Martha and Amelia tryin to keep back the creek behind the barn by themselves, so we pitched in. James went over and sat down on the back porch, outa the rain, and Martha tended to his arm while the rest of us worked on the makeshift levee. Right now, night is fallin and all of a sudden the rain stopped, so Oscar, Swede, Amelia and me get the wagon out and hitch the team up to it. We go sloggin out into the field and begin to stack bales on the wagon. The work goes smooth despite the mud and muck; its back-breakin labor. Wears yuh out. After three trips, we're all four puffin like we just did the mile run.

"We probly should get some more," Oscar says, "but we gotta rest up some. If we dont, we'll cave in."

So, we go up to the house where Martha's tendin to James. She's got his arm in a sling and he's got some kinda hot broth in front of im.

"You men look like you could use something warm and nourishing. You too Amy," Martha says. "I wont ask you to come into the kitchen and help me. From the look of it, you should get the same treatment as the men."

We've all taken our boots off and are sittin by the fire in the Franklin fireplace, and she disappears into the kitchen. Theres two couches facin each other on each side a the fireplace. Opposite the fireplace between the two couches is a great big easy chair, which Oscar sits in like a king on his throne. James and Swede are sittin on one couch, Amelia and me on the

35

other. She looks at me like she wants to see inside me. She's smilin at me like I've never seen anyone smile before.

"I laid out some dry clothes for you two boys upstairs in the room you'll be staying in. You can change into them anytime you like," Martha says as she moves around the dinin room table settin it.

"I'll show you," Amelia says, takin my hand and leadin me to the stairs. Swede's not far behind us. At the top a the stairs, he goes ahead to the right like Amelia directs im. She's been holdin my hand all the way up the stairs, and as Swede goes down the hall, she holds me back and whispers in my ear,

"Come to my room after everybodys asleep. Its at the opposite end of this hall behind us." She relaxes her grip on me, and we move down the hall toward the room Swede just went into. "My parents room is right there," she says pointin to a door about five feet further down the hall. "If yer real quiet, theyll never hear yuh." She turns and leaves as I go into the bedroom where Swede is puttin on a pair a bib overalls.

The clothes Martha has set aside for us must be some of Oscar's. Since he's bigger'n me and smaller'n Swede, the overalls fit Swede tight, and they hang on me. If I thought we was a funny pair before, now I know its true. Lookin in the mirror, I see some poor little ragamuffin, scarecrow farmer-lookin kid. I'm feelin real dumb. All of a sudden I dont feel like I want Amelia to see me lookin like this, but then I think what the hell, they are dry and comfortable, which the two pair I have aint. More comfortable than Swede anyway.

36

His overalls are a tight fit. He looks like some kinda Paul Bunyan bul-gin outa his clothes.

"She wants me to go to her room after everybodys asleep. Wha'da yuh think?" I say as I roll up the cuffs a couple rolls.

"I think I'd go if it was me," he says. "She's a real swell lookin doll, a knockout."

"Maybe she'll change her mind after she sees me in this getup. I feel like a screwball."

"Well, you look like one, but the situation is yuh just cant complain. Lets go get somethin to eat. I dont think we'll be just sittin around for the rest a the night, so we'd best get some nourishment to carry us thru."

We walk outa the room and down the hall. As we get to the head a the stairs, I look down the hall to where Amelia said her room is. "Go ahead," I tell Swede. "I'll be right down," and when he goes down the stairs, I walk down the hall.

The door to her room is open, and I look in. Her furniture is simple, an oak four-poster with a chest-a-drawers to match. On the wall above the chest hangs a beveled mirror in an oak frame. A framed picture of Oscar, Martha and Amelia standin next to a Model T is on top a the dresser. She's just a little girl in the picture, and Oscar and Martha a young couple. He's wearin a double-breasted pin-striped suit and a broad brimmed fedora restin fairly high up on his forehead, not shadin his strong, clear eyes so yuh can see em lookin back at yuh. Martha's dressed in gingham. Amelia's wearin her Sunday best. Her and Martha are wearin bonnets. She's standin on the runnin board a the

37

Model T. Her arms are hangin straight down at her sides. Oscar and Martha flank her, him toward the front a the car, her toward the back. He's got his left foot firmly planted on the ground and the other restin on the runnin board next to Amelia. His right forearm's on his right knee. His left fist is set on that hip, and the arm makes a triangle on that side a his body. Amelia, that's maybe eight years old, is standin on the runnin board next to Oscar's right leg. She has a shy look on her face. Martha's on the other side, Amelia smilin at the camera. You can see that these were happier times for the family.

Next to the bed is a small nightstand with a lamp on it. I turn to go back to the stairs, and I notice to the right down a smaller, dead-end hall a ladder goin up to a loft. Must be where James is gonna be sleepin. I walk back down the hall to the stairs. When I enter the dinin room, I look at Amelia first, and she's lookin at me. God, what a look! I take my place at the table next to James.

"So, Swede says you two boys ran away from home cuz your fathers were beating yuh up," Martha says. "I think that's just terrible. You poor boys."

"Well, times are tough, yuh know," I say. "I think maybe folks are just scared cuz they aint got no money and they dont know where their next meal's comin from, and so maybe they take it out on their kids. You know what I mean?"

"It is tough times out there," Oscar says, "but I dont reckon that gives anybody call to beat up their kids."

38

ANTOINE FAROT AND SWEDE

"We're outa there now," Swede says with a big grin on his freckled face. "California here we come."

"Course, it isnt going to be all milk and honey out there either, you know," James says. "I think they-ve got a depression, too."

"But at least its warm," I say. Amelia keeps smilin that smile and lookin straight at me.

"Well, that may be true, and that may be just enough to make the place tolerable. I've never been there myself," he says. "How about you Oscar? You ever been there?"

"No, siree. I never been outa Illinois, and with Missouri and Saint Louis just down the road a piece. Been to Chicago, tho. Took the train there once. Back in twenty-seven. Went to Sears Roebuck to pick up that there Franklin fireplace." He points with his fork at the fireplace we sat around earlier. "California seems like another world to me."

"I had opportunities to go there for my employer, but I never did," James says. "Something always came up."

Hearin im say a thing like that makes me wonder again what the hell kinda job he had. He still aint really talked about it, not to us before, not to Oscar and the rest of us now. Martha got Swede to talk about us, but she didnt get James to talk about himself.

As we sit by the light a kerosene lamps with glass chimneys, a bolt of lightnin suddenly flashes our little dinin room scene into bold relief against the opposite wall. Thunder rumbles right behind it, first with a crack followed by a long drum roll. The rain aint

39

started up again, so we all breathe a little easier. When we finish our dinner a chicken, corn bread and soup, Oscar suggests that we all hit the hay cuz we'll probly be fightin that creek again before daybreak. The women clear away the table and stack the dishes next to the kitchen water pump. We men go out onto the porch and have a look across the front yard at the creek with three rows a hay bales runnin twenty feet along its length where the bank's low. Everything's quiet in a scary way. We turn to go back into the house, and lightnin strikes again.

"About five miles away. Gettin closer," Oscar says when the thunder cracks a few seconds later.

When we get to the rooms we're supposed to be sleepin in, we run into some problems. James has trouble gettin up the ladder to his loft cuz a his arm, so he goes in with Swede, and I go to his loft. What a convenient switch that was. Amelia and me will be all by ourselves at one end a the house. My loft is warm as fresh toasted bread. Its right above the parlor where the Franklin fireplace is, and the warm chimney pipe runs up thru the center a the loft not far from the bunk I'm gonna be sleepin in. Also, it seems like all the heat in the rest a the house eventually rises to this loft. Not long after the last light is doused and the rest a the household goes silent, Amelia climbs up my ladder and is in the bunk beside me with nothin on.

"I couldnt wait for you to come down. Besides its warmer up here than in my room," she says, "and if daddy catches us, he cant put any a the blame on you."

She snuggles up to me, and takes off my under shirt and shorts, so now we *both* have nothin on. This

40

is the first time for me, and its swell. Swede told me about the first time he did it, and from the way he talked, it didnt sound like he had a good time a-tall. He said he'd done it when he was only fourteen with a girl from school named Marie. Theyd been at her house on the davenport in the parlor, and they didnt have much time cuz Marie's mom was comin home pretty soon. He said they didnt even get all their clothes off, and he really didnt get inside her. And when he was all done, he said he was sore. This wasnt nothin like that.

"I'll be right back," she says before we get started. She slips outa bed and into her robe, and before I know it, she has scrambled down the ladder and down the hallway to the stairs. I can hear her pumpin water in the kitchen. A short time passes and I hear her in the hallway again. I look down my ladder and she's standin at the bottom holdin a bucket a water up to me. I take the pan from her, and she disappears down the hall again, comin back seconds later with a towel and a bar of Ivory soap. Cuz we'd worked so hard against the creek, we was all so exhausted afterwards that we really didnt take proper baths. We'd all gone to bed pretty dirty. Amelia didn't. At some point durin the evenin, she'd cleaned up and put on some perfume she said she got from the Sears mail order catalogue. She brought the water up to my loft to clean me up. The water's pretty cool, but its okay cuz its so warm in the loft. She dont even finish washin me up before we're lost in each other's embrace, and then it happens, and God! I feel like I died and went to heaven. We actually do it a couple times before we both fall asleep naked and tired in each other's arms.

41

Five

At around three in the mornin, the rain starts hittin the roof right above us. Amelia stirs on her side a my bunk. She snuggles up to me and gives it up one more time. By the time we finish, the rains comin down pretty hard. It even sounds like it might be hail-in.

She finally pulls herself outa the bunk, wraps her robe around her and climbs down the ladder. As she's goin into her room, I hear Oscar shoutin down by the head a the stairs. He's tryin to get everybody awake so we can all go fight that river again. Then I hear im goin down the stairs. I hear James and Swede movin around, too. I get outa bed and into my own clothes, which in this warm, dry loft have got prit'near, dry. I climb down the ladder, noticin right away how much cooler it is outside my loft. I meet James and Swede at the head a the stairs, and when we start down, Amelia comes along right behind us, dressed and ready to go to work against the creek. Course I aint quite sure what we're gonna do now. There aint no more bales to stack. We could shift some from up stream to the bottom end a the levee we put up. Approachin the front door, we see the rain is comin down like a cloudburst.

"Its rainin hammer handles, aint it?" Oscar says when we join im on the front porch.

"Boy, what a storm," James says agreein with im.

ANTOINE FAROT AND SWEDE

"If this keeps up, we'll be flooded sure, and there aint a gall dang thing we can do about it neither," Oscar says. "First time I ever wished the temperature'd drop. If it would, maybe we could get some snow instead a this infernal rain. Ice up the river."

We can actually see the river risin up stream from where we built the levee a hay. The levee's still pretty solid, but you can see it aint gonna last if that river rises another couple feet, and if this rain keeps up, thatll be pretty soon. We follow Oscar down the steps and across the front yard, tiltin into the storm, to where we stacked the bales. The lower end a the levee is startin to come loose at the bottom bend a the river. If we don't shore it up, its gonna give way pretty quick. Oscar workin with Swede, and Amelia workin with me, we start to move the bales at the top upper end to the bottom lower end a the barrier until its balanced and the waters runnin (and risin) evenly along it. And that's pretty much it. Aint a whole hell of a lot we can do now. Just sit back and hope the rain stops. Whoever said the darkest hour is just before dawn sure knew what he was talkin about. Its around five-thirty, six oclock and daybreak is on the way, and its darker now than it was when we started.

In the meantime, we go into the house and start movin furniture upstairs. I guess Oscar and Martha are figurin on the worst. We move one a the couches, Oscar's chair and the sideboard into their bedroom. The other couch and the dinin room set go into the room James and Swede are stayin in. The dinin room hutch and the plates and cups in it and the Victrola go into Amelia's room. An oak ice box from the kitchen and a low coffee table that separated the two couches go in the upstairs hall, and the downstairs is pretty much cleared out. Upstairs is really crowded now. After we get everything moved, we all go downstairs and out onto the porch to watch the storm and see what damage its gonna do. Oscar goes to the barn and sets the animals loose, and they go to higher ground behind the house. He comes back to the porch to watch the storm with us.

At dawn the river takes out the top row a bales and the water rushes over the front yard toward the house. Oscar stuffs some towels along the threshold of the back door from the outside, and then he climbs thru the window back inside the house; he already did the front door when we was movin furniture. We go up a few steps where Martha and Amelia are sittin, and as I get to about the fifth step, the water starts oozing in at the threshold a the back door. We all stay on the staircase and watch helpless the water comin in. Fortunately, the house is on a solid concrete foundation, so it aint goin nowhere, and those solid doors aint gonna break open neither and let the flood in unchecked. It just oozes thru the towels at the threshold until theres a couple inches a water in the front room. The only good thing happenin right now is that the rain stopped almost at the same time the river overflowed, but it looks like its gonna be a while before these waters'll go down, even if the rain dont start up again, which none of us can predict and that's a sure thing. The water seems to of stopped risin inside the house at about two inches, so we roll our trouser legs up and go down the stairs and wade into it. Feelin this squishy stuff oozin

44

up between my toes, I all of a sudden get this real mournful feelin for Martha, knowin what a son of a bitch its gonna be for her to clean it all up. My ma's image flashes in my mind, too. I aint thought about her for a while, and it kinda makes me sad to be doin' it now.

We walk over to the front window and look out onto a lake. The water level outside is a couple inches higher than it is inside, but I expect thatll level out pretty quick. As Martha comes down the stairs, she gasps and puts her hand to her mouth. She's shocked at the sight of her house under water. And who can blame her? Right now, there aint a damn thing we can do about it, and the feelin of not havin any power a-tall seems to have beaten Martha. Oscar goes outside to check on the animals, and the rest of us go upstairs where its dry. We all go into Swede's and James's room and sit down on the couch and in the chairs around the dinin room table. Martha looks so pa-thetic and miserable.

As we're sittin around, she suddenly comes outa her misery.

"We'll just wait for the water to go down and then clean up the mess. That's all there is to it."

She seems to be holdin back her tears. She stands up and starts pacin, makin her plans out loud. This goes on for about a half hour. The rest of us just sit there and let her go on. I think a Ma again. Oscar comes back in from outside.

"The animals are okay. They went up to the high ground behind the house."

Jerome Arthur

We look out the window of our upstairs room and we can see two cows and two horses grazin on a mound that looks like a small island in the middle of a lake.

"Chickens're roosting as high up in their co-ops as they can git," Oscar says. "Theyre okay. I built them coops up high on purpose. I guess all we can do now is wait for the water to go down and then clean up. I see blue sky out there in the distance, so I'm hopin maybe this rain is done with."

By one oclock the sun has come out, peakin thru the puffy white clouds that have replaced the gray, rainy ones. Theres still about a foot a water in the yard, and the river's ragin along, but the water has all gone outa the house leavin about an inch a mud on the floor in every room downstairs. Oscar goes out to a lean-to next to the barn and wheels a wheelbarrow out with three shovels in it. Me and him and Amelia start to shovel the mud outa the parlor, and Swede wheels it out and dumps it off the edge a the porch where it splashes into the water below. James still cant do much, so he helps Martha move things around upstairs so we wont be stumblin over em. Its probly gonna be at least a day before we'll be able to move the furniture back downstairs. We work like this most a the after-noon, and eventually all that's left is a light coating of mud that can be mopped up. The water level has dropped and you can see all the weeds and grass in the yard again. The ground is still pretty muddy, so its hard to just go out into the yard.

We managed to get the kitchen pretty cleaned up, so by sundown, Martha starts cookin a meal. Aint

46

nothin fancy. She heats up yesterday's left-over chicken and opens up a couple cans a soup. Good thing Oscar keeps a supply a firewood stacked on the porch. We'll be warm tonight, and Martha can cook a meal. We're all so tired and hungry after our day's work that we wolf down our food, and since theres no place to sit next to the fire, we go straight upstairs and fall into bed tired and beat. Much to my surprise, Amelia comes up to my loft again. This girl dont seem to get tired, which is okay with me. I like this, and its even better the second night. I'm wonderin how she learned to do all this, livin way out here in the middle a nowhere.

"Where'd you learn this?" I ask her after the first time. "You have a boyfriend from one a these other farms around here or from in town?"

"No," she says. "Right around the time I took biology in school and learned about what people do to get babies, I started feelin the desire. I had my first wet dream when I was fourteen. It really wasnt wet. For boys its wet; for girls its just a feelin. I knew the boy in the dream, so I just went to im the next time I saw im in school and told im about the dream, and one thing led to another, and next I know he's on top a me in his daddy's hay loft. We was the same age. He moved away the next year. There've been a couple other boys. That's it."

She says this last with a shrug. Then before I can say or ask anymore, I'm lost in her embrace again. She stays with me almost the whole night, leavin early in the mornin, before her parents start stirrin, and we do it each time one or the other of us wakes in the night.

47

Six

I wake up in the middle a the night. I dont hear a sound in the house. Its still real dark out, so I cant see that Amelia aint in the bunk next to me. I stretch my arm across to her side. Theres nothin there but a hollow dent in the pillow where her head was. I wanted to cup her soft tits in my hands, but theyre missin and so's she. Theyre soft as Jell-O, but it aint quite the same kinda soft. I aint never felt no kinda softness that compares to Amelia's tits. And I dont get a feel this mornin cuz she's already gone. I'm listenin for more rain and cant hear none. That's a good sign. I can hear movement down toward Amelia's room. I get outa the bunk and climb half way down the ladder when I see a light flickering thru her open door. The rest a the house is dark and quiet, and it sounds like everybody else is still asleep.

I climb the rest a the way down and pad up to her room in my socks. As I come up to the door, which is wide open, I see she's settin clothes and stuff out next to a cardboard suitcase on her bed. It looks like she's packin, like maybe she's gonna take a trip or somethin. I go ahead on into the room, and she turns, a little surprised, when I come up behind her.

"I rolled over, and you was gone," I say. Then glancin at the suitcase and the clothes next to it, I ask, "Whatre yuh doin'?"

ANTOINE FAROT AND SWEDE

"I'm leavin here," she says, walkin over and closin the door. "I hate this place, and I've just got to get away from here. I wanna go with you fellas. Tell me I can."

"I'm not the only one to ask," I say.

It might be a real nice thing for me, but I know it'd be impossible for her to travel with us. We keep this up, she's liable to get knocked up. She may already be. And what would we do with a girl out on the rails, anyway? Specially a pregnant one. Just the fact she thinks she can take a suitcase with her shows she dont know nothin bout hoppin freights. She has such a pleadin look on her face that I dont have the heart to tell her what I'm thinkin. I also like her and care for her, so I know it aint gonna be easy when I *do* have to go.

"I'm in with Swede and James, so why dont we go talk to em, see what they think. We aint leavin right away anyway. We gotta stick around long enough to get yer ma and pop dug out some."

She seems to wanna keep on packin, but she stops when I turn to go back up to the loft. She blows out her lamp and follows me to the warmth of my loft. When we climb into the bunk, we get as close as man and woman can get, and I'm not even really a man yet. She's definitely a woman. Theres no doubt about that. We get lost in each other, and its swell.

Somewhere between asleep and awake I hear a rooster crow. At the sound Amelia gets outa bed, slides down the ladder and goes silently back into her room. Shortly after that, I hear Oscar come outa his room and go downstairs. I'm wonderin if he's got it figured out

49

or not. He must, but why aint he pissed off? Maybe he's just weary, beat down from this hard country life, and maybe he just aint got the pep no more to do what he thinks he should do. He aint the upright young man he was in the family picture on Amelia's dresser. To see Oscar now next to the picture, you wouldnt know he was the same man. Now, in his drooping bib overalls, he looks hunched and crooked. Its almost like he's saggin under his own weight. He keeps ploddin on, and they *do* have a pretty nice spread here. Its tough cuz its tough everywhere. He raises his crops, but nobody's got money to buy em.

Soon as I get outa bed and get dressed, I climb down the ladder and walk down the hall to the room Swede and James are in. The door's open, and theyre awake, Swede in bed on his back with his fingers laced together behind his head, and James dressed and sittin at the dinin room table. As I enter the room, closin the door behind me, I motion for Swede to join me and James at the table. We're huddled close together, and I say real quiet like, makin sure I aint overheard,

"Amelia wants to go with us when we hit the road. I told her we'd have to wait and see what you two fellas had to say. So, what're we gonna do?"

"Well, do you want her to come?" James asks.

I think he knows the answer to that one. Even if I wanted her to come, we still couldnt take her, and I think James knows that. Swede aint sayin nothin.

"Naw. We cant take her and you know it. Right? I mean she was packin a suitcase. What's that tell yuh?"

ANTOINE FAROT AND SWEDE

"That's right, but I wanted to hear you say it. We're gonna have to figure out some way to get outa here quietly and gracefully without saying goodbye and without them even knowing we're gone until we're down the road a ways. I hate to do it like that, but I dont see any other way. If Amelia's got it in her head to come with us, she'll surely do it, no matter what we or her parents say to her."

"When'll we do it?" Swede says. This is the first he's said anything.

"In a day or so," James says. "We've got to help Oscar and Martha clean up some more, and Swede and I should let our injuries mend a bit more. Couple of days oughta do it, and then we'll go. We're also gonna have to case it out, find out what's the best way to make an exit. Leave it to me. I've had experience with this kind of thing before."

We go downstairs and Oscar and Martha are scrubbin the wood floor in the kitchen and dinin room. Its barely daybreak, so Oscar goes out to tend to his chores while Swede and me help Martha clean the floor, and James and Amelia get a fire goin in the kitchen stove and start cookin a breakfast of omelet and hash browns and toasted, homemade, whole wheat bread. The kitchen and dinin room floors are tile and theyre cleanin up real easy. When we finish the dinin room, we go upstairs and bring the table and chairs down and set em up. Amelia sets the table, and Martha goes out to the front porch and clangs the triangle hangin there. We all clean up at the kitchen pump as James sets the steamin food on the table. Oscar comes

51

in with a can a fresh, warm milk. He cleans up, and we all sit down to breakfast.

"Looks like them boards in the parlor are bucklin," Oscar says. "I think theyll go back down when they dry out all the way."

"Creek ever overflow here before?" James asks.

"Nope. We been farming here for goin on seven years, and that creek never got that high before. Course, we been havin a lotta rain this early in the season. Just aint got very cold, so none of its turnin to snow, and the ground's not freezin. That oughta be happenin pretty quick now. Couple weeks till winter starts."

"That creek's overflowed before. It just never got in the house," Martha says. "Happened once in spring with the snow runoff. Wasnt even raining at the time. It just swole up and overflowed."

"That's a fact," Oscar says. "But that overflow wasnt hardly enough to even water the yard."

And so, the talk goes thru breakfast, and for a time, my eyes wander out the dinin room window toward the gravel high road we followed to get here. The gravel road goes over to a county road that runs beside the railroad tracks. I expect thatll be the one we'll take. Either that or we'll follow the tracks. God knows how far we'll have to hike to get to a spot where a trainll slow down enough for us to hop on.

It sure is different havin milk that's warm right outa the cow. After breakfast, Martha clears the dishes, and her and Amelia start washin em. Swede joins Oscar, helpin im with the livestock, and gettin the barn

52

ready for winter. Me and James go to work on the parlor floor. His arm's doin' a lot better. As we're scrubbin, he says to me in a low voice,

"As soon as we finish in here, I'm gonna take
a walk back to the railroad line, see what that road
looks like, and then I'll talk to Oscar, find out what
towns lie south of here and how far away they are.
Maybe we can get outa here sometime early tomorrow
afternoon."

"Boy, that sure sounds good to me," I say.
"Winter's on the way. First this rain; snow's next. We
gotta get away from this weather."

We keep moppin up mud for a couple hours,
dumpin buckets of muddy water out in the yard. James
gets his jacket on and walks out the front door and
down the steps to the yard. As I'm doin' the last mop
up, I watch im walk off across the yard to the road, and
then he disappears around the bend as he heads toward
the railroad tracks. In the meantime, Amelia finished
the dishes and cleanin up the kitchen She took James's
place and is helpin me mop the parlor floor. The only
floors that still need to be cleaned are the service porch
and the front porch. Martha starts on the service porch,
leavin me alone with Amelia to do the front porch. As
soon as we begin, she starts askin me what James and
Swede said about her goin along with us. I stall her,
tellin her that I aint had a chance to talk to em, and she
gets a disappointed look on her face.

"If you dont ask em, we'll never find out if its
okay for me to go," she says. "Please ask em, Antoine.
I dont feel like I can stay her another day."

"I know you dont, but I aint so sure you wanna hop a freight to do it. Its a hard life ridin the rails. You'd be the only girl. There just aint no others. You aint never gonna be any colder. You wont have yer nice warm bed to jump into at night."

"I know it wont be easy, but I figure once I get to California, I can maybe get a job, maybe even try to be a movie star. I just know I've gotta get outa here."

I dont know what more I can say to her, so I dont say nothin. I think I already said too much. She's probly guessed from what I just said that we dont wanna take her with us. She's lookin at me like she's ready to ask me for a straight answer, but she dont. I guess she thinks I want her to go and I'll argue for her against James and Swede. Well, if that's what she thinks, I guess that's a good deal. At least it saves me from havin to look her straight in the eye and to tell her I dont want her to come with us. It would hurt me to hurt her like that. But its the only honest way. I guess I'll just have to be dishonest cuz I know I couldnt face her with that kinda bad news.

Its gettin on to late afternoon when we finish the porch. James still aint come back from his little scoutin trip. Amelia joins Martha in gettin things ready for dinner. I walk out to the barn to see what Swede and Oscar are doin', but as I approach the barn door, theyre comin out wipin their hands. They done all theyre gonna do for the day. As we head back to the house, James comes in from the gravel road.

"Well, where you been at?" Oscar asks.

"Oh, I was just out exploring your territory around here," James says. "How far is the next town

54

south of here, or I should say, the next town where a freight train might stop?"

"That'd be Cairo, about thirty-five miles due south a here. Did yuh see the county road runnin alongside the tracks? Well, that takes yuh to Anna about four miles, and from there yuh go another mile to Jonesboro where theres a pretty good paved highway with quite a bit a truck traffic. Crops goin to market. I'd bet you boys could probly hitch a ride real easy on one a them trucks. Once you get to Cairo, you could decide if you wanna go by rail or by raft, that is if yuh could find a raft. You boys got any money?"

"Just three dollars," James says.

"Well, I dont reckon yuh can get one for that, but yuh could ask around? You boys aint plannin on leavin us already, are yuh? Hell, I was just gettin used to the idea of havin y'all around."

"Not yet, but you know we cant stay forever," James says.

"Well, I know, but you fellas have been a real help around here, and I'm a gonna miss yuh when yuh go."

This makes me feel guilty for how we're plannin on leavin. When we go into the house, we're hit by the aroma of ham bakin in the oven. Theres fires in both the kitchen and parlor stoves, and the house is warm and toasty. Its still damp tho, but I think itll dry out pretty quick with these fires. While we wait for the ham to finish cookin, we move the rest a the furniture down from upstairs. When we finish that chore, we still have a few minutes before the ham will be done, so we sit down by the fire.

"So, whatre yer travelin plans?" Oscar asks. Amelia perks up and is paying attention to our conversation as she sets the table and helps Martha in the kitchen. James notices this, and I see he's bein cagey as he answers.

"Well, I cant say when we'll be leaving, if you dont mind our staying for just a while longer. I think my arm needs a little more time to mend. As far as our travelin plans are concerned, I think we'll just follow your advice and try to hitch a ride to Cairo, then hop a freight from there."

"Come and get it," Martha says, settin the ham in the center a the table.

We all get up and go over to the dinin room table, which is decked out like the holidays. It almost seems like we're celebratin our leavin, but only half of us know it.

"I got the ham out to celebrate our good fortune at havin y'all wander in on us the way you did the other day," Martha says. "I had it stored up in salt, and thought it was time to get it out and share it."

"Well, it sure looks good, ma'am," Swede says.

And then we're all eatin. I cant believe I'm eatin lean pork and not just gristle. It tastes good and I say,

"This is the best ham I ever had. It melts right in yer mouth, dont it?"

"Boy, I'll say," James says. Then we fall silent and eat our dinner.

Afterward the men walk out onto the front porch while the women pick up the dishes and take em into the kitchen to wash em. Its freezin cold outside and we dont stay out there long, just long enough to look over the yard and barn, and then we go back into the parlor and sit by the fire. The women join us when they finish the dishes. We only sit there for about a half hour, not talkin about much, listenin to James on his harmonica, and then we head up to our rooms. About a half hour after the house goes quiet and everybody's asleep, Amelia climbs up my ladder and is in bed with me. After the first time she says to me,

"Well, what did James and Swede say when you told them I wanted to go with you?"

"Well, uh, er, uh they said its gonna take a little plannin, so its gonna take some time to think it out," I lie, but I just cant do nothin else.

"Oh, so they didnt just refuse outright then?" she says. "That's some encouragement."

I dont say no more. I fall asleep and dont wake up again until she wakes me to do it again. When the rooster crows again just before dawn she glides back down to her room, and I fall back to sleep and dont wake up again until well past sunrise.

Seven

I get outa the bunk and look out the little dormer window and see a thin dusting of snow on the ground and in the bare branches of the trees. It aint a heavy snow (more of a heavy frost) and in fact its icin up and meltin in the sun. Oscars crossin the yard to the barn. Even from this high up I hear his boots crunchin on the frozen ground. What a difference from just the day before yesterday when he went sloggin off in his rain boots in two feet a water. I put my trousers and shirt on and climb down the ladder and go down the hall to see what James and Swede are up to. They aint in their room, but I hear em downstairs, and I can smell breakfast. When I walk into the dinin room, all of em except Oscar, who went out to the barn to tend to the animals, are sittin around the dinin room table havin bacon and eggs and hot coffee and warm milk. That's one thing about bein a farmer durin a depression. You can at least raise yer own food as long as the land holds out and the bank dont have a mortgage against it. Everything on the table except the coffee came from the land or an animal raised on the land.

I join em at the table. Martha gets up and goes into the kitchen and fixes some fresh scrambled eggs and a couple strips a bacon for me. When she leaves, the conversation at the table goes silent. I sense some tension between Amelia and James. Then James says in a low voice,

ANTOINE FAROT AND SWEDE

"Amelia here brought up what we talked about yesterday. I told her its gonna take some time to work it out, and she seems to think I'm putting her off."

"Well you are, arent you?" she says. "What does it take? We leave in the night, and that's it. We're gone. How complicated is that?"

"Shhh," I say. Her voice rises with her last question.

"We can talk about it later," James says. "I'm workin it out right now."

Just then Martha calls Amelia into the kitchen, and as soon as she's outa hearin, James says to us quick and quiet,

"We're outa here today after lunch. We'll leave one at a time. Just slip out the best way you can. We'll meet in Anna, four miles down the road." He points south.

Amelia comes back into the dinin room with a plate of food and a glass a milk for me. She sets em in front a me and sits down. Her mother comes in from the kitchen. I'm the only one still eatin. They was all finishin when I came in. They got up pretty late too, but it was a little earlier than me. Oscar, course, was awake before daybreak, but Martha says he didnt get outa bed right away. Now theyre in the season when there aint much to do except tend to the animals, and pretty soon when it starts snowin, theyre gonna be pretty much house bound. That even happened to us in Minneapolis. If we got a heavy snow storm, people couldnt go to work and school the next day, and the only thing you could do would be to stay in the house. Cuz it was warm there, it was the best place to be, but with Wiktor Sadlo stuck there too, I usually wound up goin out anyway. After livin my whole life in Minneapolis, I never did get used to the cold winters. Sometimes I think someone got somethin mixed up when I was born. As thick as my blood is, and as little and skinny as I am with not much fat for insulation, there must be some mistake that I should be born and be livin in a place like Minneapolis.

James's and Swede's injuries seem to be gettin better and better. The swellin in Swede's wrist has disappeared altogether. He says its still a little tender, so he's careful with it, but otherwise he's back to normal. James has removed his arm from the sling and he's almost got full movement with it.

Theres still some mud and even a couple feet a water in the cellar, so we start a bucket brigade, and an hour later we're down to mud only. We spend about another hour on it and the mud is cleaned up, too. After this job, I can honestly say we earned our keep here.

"First time I had to do this was when I got the Franklin from Sears," Oscar says. "You can see the coal furnace got completely flooded out; its happened before." A wrinkled layer a mud drips mourn-ful from the spout a the coal chute. "Whoever built this place, built her solid, but he built her down too low. He shoulda put her up on the hill where the animals graze, but since he decided on the meadow next to the creek, he should never a put no cellar in. Cant hardly use it."

We been workin pretty hard the last couple days, and its been dirty work, too. Course the bonus for me here was Amelia. I know I'm gonna miss her. Maybe I'll write to her whenever I get settled somewhere. Send her a postcard from Hollywood. I wouldnt even mind it if she wanted to come out and stay with me once I get settled in a job and get a place to live. But that remains to be seen. Right now, I gotta figure out how I'm gonna get away from her without her knowin I'm gone.

At around noon Martha and Amelia go to the kitchen and put together a lunch a hot Campbells tomato soup, and bacon, lettuce and tomato sandwiches. Since this is gonna be our last good meal for who knows how long, I'm really gonna enjoy it. I've still got the three-fifty in my coat linin, and I'm sure when we get to some town down the line, we'll be able to buy some good food and eat pretty good for a while. I dont know how far we are from New Orleans. That's our next goal. Seein snow on the ground this mornin really makes me wanna get there in a hurry.

When we finish lunch, James tells Oscar he's gonna take a walk, maybe go as far as Anna, just to look it over to get an idea where we'll be goin from here. Swede and me understand this to be our cue to get our stuff together and high tail it outa here soon as we can after he's gone. The three of us go upstairs and close the door. James gathers up his stuff and puts as much in his pockets as he can; he mixes the rest of it with Swede's and my things and tells us to bring it with us when we sneak out. He says it might look too obvious if he went off for a walk carryin all his stuff. Swede goes downstairs to hang around with Oscar, Martha and Amelia, and I go up to my loft to get my stuff together. When I get it all tied up in the bedroll, I open the dormer window and drop it out. Theres some

61

bushes right straight down, and it falls into em and hides there. I climb down the ladder, walk down the hall and go downstairs where Swede and the family are sittin in the parlor talkin.

"Where's James?" I ask, all innocence.

"Went out for a walk," Oscar says. "I reckon he's takin a likin to our part a the country here, the way he's been explorin around."

"I think that's wishful thinking, Papa," Amelia says. The gloom showin in her face pains me. I wish we could take her away from here, but it just aint possible.

"Why, honey, it isnt so bad," Martha says. Its pretty plain she knows Amelia's unhappy. You can tell they had this conversation before.

"After all that's happened these last few days, I dont see how you can say that, Mama. Three feet deep in water one day and snow the next, and more snow from now on. Breaking our backs raising crops and not being able to sell them. Not to mention the boredom."

It fairly breaks my heart to hear her talk so, cuz I know she's right, and I think Martha knows she's right, too, but she cant admit it to herself cuz if she did, she could never justify any of em stayin here. All they have is the farm and each other.

"That all may be true," says Oscar, "but this here place provides us with food and shelter, and I bet you aint gonna find that in too many places in these hard times. The rich get richer, and the poor get poorer, and I dont think I have to tell yuh which one a those we are."

62

ANTOINE FAROT AND SWEDE

I know how right he is. I aint even been on the road a week yet, and I've had a small taste a bein without a home and hungry. Amelia dont know it, but she's got it pretty good here, yet I can understand her complaints. Oscar finally stands up to go outside. He looks like a man that's been thru this conversation before, and he has spoken and dont wanna talk about it no more. Without another word he walks outa the room, and we hear the back-door slam shut as he heads toward the barn.

"We better get busy, and churn some butter, Amy," Martha says.

They get up and follow Oscar out the back door. We can hear em settin up the churn.

"My bedroll's in the bushes on the side a the house," I say. "Alls I gotta do is pick it up and start walkin."

"Well why dont you go ahead and get it and get goin," Swede says. "I'll go up and get my stuff ready and be on my way in a little while. I'll go out and help Oscar a little more in the barn before I leave."

I go out the front door and around the side a the house. My bedroll's right where I dropped it, so I dig it out and look around to make sure nobody's watchin me. Then I scamper across the yard and take cover behind a tree. From there I'm lookin at the front a the house with the barn in the yard behind it. No one in sight. Amelia and Martha are in the service porch churnin. Oscar's still in the barn. I duck outa the yard and into some bushes beside the creek. Theres about twenty-five feet separatin me from the bend in the lane that leads outa here. I scurry over there without bein seen and I'm on my way. Once I get past the bend yuh cant see me from the house or barn. I take one look back only to see an empty space in my future cuz I'll probly never see Amelia again.

I dont see a soul until I get about a mile south on the county road, when a horse drawn cart approaches ahead. As he gets abreast a me, I ask im if I'm goin in the right direction to get to Anna. He says yes, and says I got about another three miles to go. Then he's on his way, and I keep on walkin. I dont see another soul until I get to the outskirts a town where occasionally a woman walks out a front door and goes into the center a town to the general store. I'm walkin pretty fast so I get there within less than a couple hours. I find James talkin to the mechanic in a fillin station just off the main street in town. From the way theyre talkin, it sounds like they got friends in common in Chicago. I think that's what theyre talkin about when I come up to em, but James clams up as soon as I show up, so I cant be sure.

"Antoine, Joey here's gonna get us a ride to Cairo," he says as he introduces me to the mechanic.

"Swell," I say. "When?"

"Not till morning. Tonight, we gotta go into Jonesboro. We'll leave from there in the morning. Joeys gonna drive us over there after Swede gets here. Lets just keep an eye out now."

So, we stay put for a while. Every so often I walk up to the corner to check on Swede. He finally shows up at twilight time.

64

Eight

We found an old abandoned Chevy panel wagon in a vacant lot in Jonesboro, and we spent the night, three across, in the back of it. This town's a little smaller'n the other one. I'd call it more a village. Anna had a main downtown street with a general store, a movie theater, a fillin station with a garage, and a bank. By comparison Jonesboro's only a weigh station for trucks takin crops to market in Cairo. The only thing that makes it a legit town is that its the county seat and its got a courthouse and a war memorial. Joey's supposed to meet us at eight oclock and set us up with a ride to Cairo in a movin van. I'm not sure what it is, but somethin about Joey gives me the willies. He looks like a shady character. I wouldnt be surprised if he had mob connections. I wonder how James got hooked up with im. I wonder even more why James got so close to im. He really does like the guy. I dont trust im as much as James does. In fact, I even have a feelin of danger when he's around, like he's trouble lookin for some place to happen, and I dont wanna be in the middle of it when it does happen. He aint like Mousey, where you just dont like im outright; Joey's likable enough; its his attitude and the feelin that somethin bad's gonna happen.

The three of us are awake when the sun peaks over the eastern horizon. The days are gettin shorter as we get closer to the change a season. Its the first week in December which makes it only two and a half weeks away from the first day a winter. Last night was the coldest one so far. Its a good thing we was inside the car; we was warmer cuz of it. The lot where the car sits is littered with stuff people have been dumpin: an old davenport, a mangled wooden baby's crib, some dried out bushes someone trimmed back and dumped there. We manage to gather up enough junk to get a fire goin. We huddle next to it with our backs to the sun. We manage to get a little warm that way. When I look at how miserable we are, it makes me glad we didnt bring Amelia along with us. How could we ever have done this with her? I know the Polack would be happy as hell if he could see what a sorry son of a bitch I turned out to be. There aint no doubt he'd see the whole situation as typical a me. It *is* pitiful, but it aint nothin like what he may think it is. At least these fellas are all good people. They damn sure treat me better'n he ever did. I wonder how Ma's doin'. I sure hope he aint mad at her for what I done to im and is takin it out on her since he aint got me to take it out on. If he does, I swear I'll kill the son of a bitch. Hell, listen to me. For all I know, I already did kill im, and he may be too dead to take anything out on anybody.

Joey shows up at eight oclock in the great big old black Pierce-Arrow he brought us here in last night. If anything would make you think he was hooked up with mobsters, that car would. When he pulls up in it, you half-ass expect some tough guy with a heavy top-coat and a wide-brim fedora to step outa the back seat, but that aint what happens. Instead he's dressed in the same work clothes he was wearing yesterday and tells us all to get in. Then he drives to a warehouse on the southern outskirts a town. A movin van is backed up to a loadin dock and some fellas are movin furniture into it. One man has a clipboard and he seems to be in charge. Joey walks up to im. We follow.

"These are the three men I told you about last night," he says to the man in charge. "Theyre gonna help yuh finish loadin up here, and then yer gonna take em down to Cairo, right?"

"Right," he says to Joey. Then to us, "Okay, you boys start movin that furniture from the warehouse and get it loaded on the truck. These fellas'll show yuh what to do."

Now I know Joey's hooked up with gangsters; no doubt in my mind that this guy's one. So, we start loadin this real expensive lookin, fancy furniture onto a real fancy truck. Theres velvet sofas and chairs, mirrors with beveled glass framed in exotic lookin hardwoods, fancy brass lamps with silk shades, and Persian rugs. And the truck we're loadin it on is real plush. I cant imagine who can possibly own such nice stuff, but to own it and to ship it some place far away seems to me the livin end in luxury. Where can they be sendin it, and why? James walks with Joey back to his car, shakes hands with im and walks back to the loadin dock as Joey drives off toward Anna.

When we get the hang a what needs to be loaded and how, the other two fellas quit, and now its only the three of us finishing up the job. Those other two fellas aint just railroad bums like us; they got jobs and homes, the whole works. They was just startin the job we would finish. James is still kinda hobbled in that one arm a his, so its clumsy goin, but we finally get the truck all loaded up, and the boss comes over and shows us how to arrange things near the tail gate so its all set up with a couple chairs and couches arranged for us to use. He throws dust covers over em and tells us that's where we'll be ridin on the trip to Cairo. Itll actually be the most comfortable way we've traveled so far. The van is a nice new one, and it should seal up real good, so itll be like relaxin in a parlor. Theres three vents in the ceilin, so there should be good airflow. And far as the furniture goes, we'll be loungin in the lap a luxury.

We all go into an office inside the warehouse where the other two men are sittin on a davenport drinkin hot coffee. A potbelly stove glows in the center a the room. Its a good size office with a big oak rolltop desk and swivel oak chair along one wall, and a davenport against the opposite wall. One a these two is the driver and the other one works in this warehouse. Theyre lucky to have such good jobs. The boss pours us all a cup a coffee and offers us a bag with some doughnuts in it. We each take one and eat it, but they aint very good, nowheres near as good as Ma's. Course these ones are strictly store bought and that's the difference right there. So, we sit and eat our doughnuts and drink our coffee. The driver, the warehouseman and the boss are all talkin about the weather, how its probly gonna be a cold winter cuz it got cold so early in the season.

"You fellas done got the right idea," the warehouseman says, "headin south. Soon's you leave Illinois, you'll notice a difference in the temperature. Get down into Tennessee and Mississippi and winters aint much different than summers. Wished I was goin, but I cant. I got a family depending on me, and I got a job, somethin hard to come by in these hard times."

"Shoot, you'd never go even if yuh could," says the truck driver. "You wouldnt know how to act outside southern Illinois."

"You got a point there," says the warehouse-man, "but I sure would like to spend one winter in some place like Florida or California just to see what its like. Hell, I was down to New Orleans once in the wintertime. It was real warm."

"You'd probly complain about it bein too hot after a while," the other one says.

You can tell he's just needlin the warehouse-man, tryin to get a rise outa him, but the warehouseman aint budgin. Actin like he didnt hear the remark, he says in a calm and even voice,

"Yep, it was plenty warm down there, but they sure got a lot a colored folks, and they dont treat em any too good neither. They got special places for em to sit at in the back a streetcars, and the coloreds have their own public toilets and drinkin fountains. They cant drink at fountains that say 'white.' And then all of em, colored and white, talk funny as hell. Slow drawlin all the time."

These here fellas talk kinda funny far's I'm concerned. Kinda like they got a mouth full a mush. Just the way they pronounce the word Cairo. They say Kayrow. Who knows, maybe they talk even funnier the further down south we go.

69

"So, what time we gonna be pullin out?" James says.

"Yeah, I suppose we better be gettin on it," the trucker says. "Its almost eleven oclock now, and we gotta get this stuff to Cairo by one."

So, we all stand up and shuffle around for a minute or two and then walk on out to the truck. James gets into the cab with the driver, and me and Swede climb into the van and close the door behind us. The driver gives us a flashlight which is kinda nice, but we do have a little light comin in thru the three air vents up near the ceilin. We hear the motor kick in and in a short time we're rollin. We actually dont even turn the flashlight on. Instead we curl up on a couple couches and go to sleep. This is the most comfortable I've been since the loft, so I'm gonna take advantage of it. I unwrap my bedroll and curl up with my army blanket and sleep soundly and dont wake up till I dont feel the whine of the highway underneath us, and the truck comes to a stop. I reach over and grab the flashlight and shine it on the door latch. Swede releases the latch, and sunlight washes in and fills the van when the doors swing open. I have to put my hand up to shade my eyes from it.

We're parked next to a dock on the river. Theres a river boat with a huge paddle wheel at the back tied up at the dock. As we walk around the side a the truck, we meet James who got outa the cab as soon as the truck stopped. He's starin at the boat, as we are too, awestruck. Its huge, and you can tell even from this distance that its all plush and deluxe and first class.

70

ANTOINE FAROT AND SWEDE

"This is where the furniture gets unloaded," the truck driver says.

"What do you mean?" James asks. "Where do we put it?"

"On the boat," says the truck driver. "I understand some mob boss from up Chicago owns it. One a Capone's boys. He wants his furniture on it. Says he wants to cruise the river for a while. Get away from it all."

"What's his name?" James says. I notice some tension in his voice when he asks the question.

"Dont know. When it comes to this kinda work, I dont ask questions. I just do the job and keep my mouth shut. Joey knows im. He's the one that set the job up for me. I guess we better get a move on and get it furnished for im."

"Is he gonna be here today?" James says.

"Not supposed to be."

"Oh, okay, then lets get goin," James says with a sigh. He seems relieved.

So, we begin to move the furniture from the truck down to the dock and up the gangplank to the riverboat. As we do it, James keeps lookin over his shoulder, peekin around corners, and scannin the dock. He's real nervous about somethin. The riverboat is real plush inside. It has wall-to-wall carpet and crystal chandeliers in the casino and saloon. Hell, it makes you wonder what theyre gonna do with the Persian rugs. It takes us a good two hours to move it all, and just as we're unloading the last few things from the truck, the owner a the boat shows up. James is in the truck as he pulls up, and as soon as he sees im, he tells me,

71

"I gotta get outa here. I'll meet you boys later at the train yard. See yuh," and before I can ask im why, he's gone, so I pull Swede aside and tell im what happened.

We move the last pieces of furniture from the truck and onto the boat. Then we go to the trucker and tell im we're done. He takes us to the owner a the boat and tells im we was the ones that moved his furniture. Its at this point that he realizes James has disappeared.

"Hey, what happened to the other fella," he says.

"Dont know," I say. "Just took off."

"Oh, well. These are the fellas that moved the furniture," he says to this heavy set, shady lookin character with a big fat stogy stickin outa his mouth.

Not sayin anything, he peels a couple five-dollar bills off a stack he's taken out of a gold money clip and gives one to Swede and one to me. Then he turns and goes up the gang plank and onto his river boat. We ask the trucker how to get to the train yard, and he offers to take us there, so we climb into the cab and wait for im to finish his business with the owner a the boat. While we're waitin, Swede gives me his five bucks and I store it and my five in the liner a my coat with the other three-fifty.

As he drives us the half-mile or so to the train yard, he keeps talkin, as if to himself, about James's sudden disappearance. We aint sayin nothin, so he just rambles along about how James was there, and then all of a sudden, he wasnt, but why had he stayed all the way to the end, but not long enough to get some cold hard cash? His questions seem legit to me. I wonder about some a those things myself. I wonder why James was so edgy while we was hangin around that boat. It was almost like he knew the owner and was tryin to not be seen by im.

As soon as we get dropped off near where the trains come thru, I can hear James's harmonica. The train station is over on our right. The sound a the mouth organ is comin from the shelter of a couple trees to our left. Funny how sweet and melancholy that sound is. I really missed hearin it. He didnt play much while we was stayin at the farm, and he didnt play it at all last night in the Chevy. I guess we'll be hearin it again now that we're back out on the rails.

Nine

On the train goin outa Cairo, we can see that the town sits on a peninsula that points south where the Ohio flows into the Mississippi. The trucker explained the lay of the land to us durin one of our breaks movin the furniture. We cross the Ohio on a trestle bridge and we're in Kentucky rollin thru open country on the rails again. Theres somethin real calm, like bein back in the womb, when yer ridin in a boxcar. Oh, no doubt about it, theres a hell of a clatter and rumble, and its noisy as hell, but its a smooth rockin ride. Last night James was tellin me and Swede about a book he read once, The Adventures of Huckleberry Finn. He said bein in Cairo made im think a the book cuz the town played a part in the story. He was tellin us how Huck, the main character, talked about raftin down the river, and how easy and slow and lazy it was, and he guessed there just couldnt be anything better in life. I think ridin the train might be. Its at least as good. Rollin down the tracks, the cars rock back and forth. Theres a constant clickety-clackin that yuh not only hear, but yuh feel, too. If yuh lay flat on yer back on the floor of a boxcar, its like layin in a hammock or rockin in a cradle, and a course yuh got complete freedom. Luckily we got a few bucks between us, so I guess yuh could say we're ridin in style. In some ways we're better off than if we was in a regular passenger car. Its a bit breezy in a boxcar, but its a lot more free and easy, and yuh cant beat the price.

The three of us are alone, which is kinda nice. We got the whole thing to ourselves, so we can get up and move around if we like. Its warm enough to keep the door cracked so we can watch the countryside roll by. It takes us about an hour to get to Fulton, Kentucky and then we cross the line into Tennessee. We're really gettin into the south now; I'm startin to see trees and plants like I aint never seen before. Those big green, hangin-lookin ones must be the weepin willows I've seen pictures of in *Life* magazine. Seems trains go thru the back side a towns a lot, and as we roll thru some a these small southern towns, we see neighborhoods that are mostly tar paper shacks and rickety shanties. Bare footed colored men wearin bib overalls with patches on em sit on porches. Laundry flaps in the breeze on clotheslines in some back yards. Big, old-lookin colored ladies bustle around sweepin and cleanin dirty and cluttered houses. Kids are everywhere, scamperin around broken front yards and in the dusty road. It dont look like much of a life. I'm sure glad I'm here and not there.

The view is only temporary as we roll past such scenes quick and head out into open country again. And that aint even a pleasant sight. You can see the land is also sufferin from the depression. What looks like rich bottom land to me is laying fallow, I guess cuz whoever owns it aint got the dough to farm it. Banks probly foreclosed on all this land cuz the people that were farmin it couldnt make the mortgage payments. That's what James says happened, and I

75

think he's right. You live in the city and you lose yer job workin for the man; you live on the farm and you lose yer land, which *is* yer job. I wonder how long this can go on. What's it gonna take to get people workin again? I dont know, that's for sure, and I bet none a them damn politicians know neither. I always have to laugh when I see a news-paper headline sayin somethin like, "HOOVER ACTS TO STEM UNEMPLOYMENT." What's he got to worry about? He still gets his paycheck. Same with all the politicians. Seems to me theyre the same crowd that gets richer while the rest of us get poorer like Oscar said.

Its early afternoon when we rumble thru Dyersburg. Dont look like theres any stoppin this train. Maybe we'll make it all the way to Memphis in one ride. Or if we get real lucky, we could get one ride to New Orleans. The temperature's a lot warmer here than it was just a couple hundred miles north a here. I dont know why that should surprise me, but it does. Somehow I thought such talk about warmer weather in the south was a lota hooey, so now that I'm really seein it, it seems too good to be true. Outside a little burg called Henning, the train stops at a water tank. We look out the door and see the train men filling a tanker with water. While we're watchin, we're startled to hear the other door slide open behind us. At first we get ready to scurry out the door we're lookin outa, thinkin maybe its some bulls or somethin, but when we turn to look, we see an old man, maybe sixty years old, and a young man in his late teens or maybe early twenties. The younger one boosts the older one up into the car, and then he scampers in behind im. Theyre standoffish and

bashful, not sayin nothin to us, but keepin to themselves, eyein us real careful.

After a few minutes, the train lurches forward,
and the younger man comes over. Meantime, the old
man has dozed off and is sleepin like a baby. The
younger one's name is Quentin Campbell and the old
man is his grandpa, Martin Campbell. Theyre on their
way to Memphis to try to hook up with one a Martin's
brothers that lives there and has a job. They came from
Calloway County, Kentucky, where they was family
farmers with Quentin's father and mother. They lost
their farm, the same one Martin had homesteaded thirty
years ago. Quentin's mom and dad moved to Louisville
to live with her brother and his wife. Quentin says him
and his grandpa got rousted off a train a few miles back
up the track, and they waited a couple hours before this
one came along.

"I guess we're lucky it stopped," he said.
"Sure made it easier for us to get on. Now I'm just
gonna keep my fingers crossed and hope we make it to
Memphis without gettin bumped again."

"That's one thing yuh can count on," Swede
says. "Yer gonna get rousted by the bulls, and yuh
never know when its gonna happen."

And it happens as we get to the outskirts a
Memphis. Just before we get to a trestle crossing a river, the train slows down. We're gettin real familiar
with the signals and that's the first one. Next we look
out the door and see men comin off the trestle and
headin our way. As the train comes to a halt, we jump
off and scramble to get away from the tracks. Theres
no place for us to take cover around here, so all we can

77

do is try to put distance between us and the bulls. Theyre not even chasin us or any a the other hobos that jumped outa the other cars. Theyre lookin into the empty boxcars and then gettin on em. Before we know it, the train is gone across the trestle and is headin on into Memphis.

We walk across the trestle, and about a half mile further on we pass an old wooden sign that says "North Memphis" on it. Right here the tracks cut across a meadow that looks to be on the edge a town. On the other side a the meadow to our left we see a huge tent, kinda like a circus bigtop, but without any other circus equipment around it. A lota people are movin toward it. They look clean and dressed up, like they might be goin to church, but some of em, the men, are wearin clean bib overalls and straw hats, and the women are wearin long, gingham dresses and sunbonnets. James suggests we go have a look. Its Wednesday afternoon about three oclock and the clouds are gatherin, so we might be in for some rain before the day is over. As we get closer to the entrance a the tent, the crowd gets thicker. Next to the tents entrance theres a framework that looks like a painter's easel with a plywood sign on it. The sign says: "WITNESS THE TESTAMENT THRU REV. JIM BOB RAY." These words arch over a glossy picture of a smilin man I guess is Jim Bob Ray. He sure looks like a snake oil salesman to me. Under the picture, it says: "RECEIVE THE LORD JESUS."

As soon as we get near the entrance, we get swept up in the crowd, and before we know it, we're inside with the rest a the congregation. We find five chairs in a row toward the back, and we sit down, which is just the right thing for Martin Campbell. He keeps up pretty good, but he seems to get more pooped out than the rest of us. The rain starts to fall outside, so we're all pretty glad we're in here, even tho we dont wanna be listenin to a sermon. I'm not even sure what the hell Jim Bob Ray is talkin about. Somethin about hell fire and damnation, and burnin in hell for our sins. And then some woman goes up to im on crutches and kneels down in front of im and after he puts his hands on her, she stands up and throws her crutches away and walks back out into the audience without even limpin. This miracle throws different groups of people into fits around the tent. Two ladies that seem to be with the cured lady all of a sudden go into spasms in the aisle between the rows of chairs. They look possessed, I dont know by what. This is supposed to be a religious meetin, but these people here look like maybe some demons got a hold of em. And then on the other hand, theres the farmer in front a me wearin bib overalls and a clean and pressed flannel shirt. The back of his neck is a cracked and weathered checkerboard like the ground durin a drought, and whenever Reverend Jim Bob Ray says somethin he thinks is important, he squeezes the shoulder of the lady next to im, I guess his wife. Its a touchin scene in the middle of all this other hocus pocus goin on here.

Reverend Jim Bob Ray rants and raves for about an hour and a half, lightnin flashin and thunder crashin in the background. About fifteen minutes before he finishes his sermon, the storm tapers off, so that by the time he quits talkin, the weather has calmed down quite a bit. The tent revival meetin turned out to be an excellent shelter from the storm. The timin was perfect. Some gospel singers start their act, and the collection baskets start goin around. Martin Campbell is hunched over sound asleep in his chair. James looks at me and Swede and gives his head a toss, motioning for us to make our exit. When we stand up, Quentin nudges his grandpa awake, and we all move toward the openin where we came in.

Comin outa the tent, we walk thru the mud back to the train tracks. The wind is blowin, and the last light is disappearin from the horizon. Its still dark and stormy lookin, but it looks like the rains let up for the night. As we hike down the track, I look back over my shoulder at the tent, and wonder how the Reverend Jim Bob Ray does it. Everywhere I look, I see hard times and a lota sufferin, but here's Jim Bob Ray wearin a hundred-dollar suit, perfectly barbered hair and diamond rings on his manicured fingers, and then theres also his entourage, gospel singers and plants in the audience that get miraculous cures. Theres also the travel, train fares and fancy hotels.

We keep hikin on into the dusk.

Followin the tracks outa the meadow, we come upon a small river on our right. On our left are some more muddy back streets lined with run down, hopeless lookin old houses. Now we get to see it up close, on foot and at a slower pace, not just slidin by framed by a boxcar door. After about three blocks of this, we're all of a sudden in regular neighborhoods like the ones back home where theres regular family houses with parlors and dinin rooms. We walk away from the tracks at Keel Avenue and go over three blocks to Third Street. It looks like the main street thru town, so we head south on it till we get to Beale Street, and all of a sudden it looks like we've reached honky tonk heaven. Boy, what an excitin place this is! I always thought those joints my dad used to hang around in were hot, but this is where the action is. Mostly colored fellas tho, but that dont bother me none. Hell, I never met a one a them fellas didnt wanna have a good time just like me and Swede. You can tell theres all kinds a stuff goin on here. We hear jazz and blues drifting outa almost every doorway we pass. I just wanna stop and listen, but we keep movin. Lota fellas hangin around, but it aint like theyre despairin from hard times and the depression. Theyre hangin around tryin to get some action goin. Theyre struttin and hobnobbin up and down the street in and outa pool halls and juke joints. The street is all lit up and gay.

Mister Campbell takes a piece a paper outa his coat pocket and unfolds it. Written in what looks like a child's scrawl is his brothers name and address: Benjamin Campbell, 304 Griffin, Memphis, Tennessee. He says,

"I reckon I better find out where this is so's me and the boy here have a place to stay tonight. We'll see what he's got; maybe therell be room for you three boys, too."

Just about then we come upon a fillin station, so we go in and talk to the attendant. He aint doin' much, so he's glad to give us directions.

"Y'all go back in the direction y'all just come from," he says, "till yuh hit Third Street. Take a left on

81

Third and go down the road a piece. About six blocks. Itll be on yer left."

Martin Campbell thanks im, and we head off back down Beale Street where we just came from. When we get to the street, we find the house, and Quentin and Martin go up and knock on the front door while James and me and Swede wait down on the sidewalk. The next-door neighbor pokes her head out her window and says,

"He wont be home till after nine oclock when his shift ends. That's a little over an hour and a half from now."

"Well, I reckon we'll just wait for im on the front porch here," Martin says. "I'm his brother Martin from Kentucky, and this is my grandson, Quentin. These men are friends we met on the trip down here."

"I guess thatll be okay," she says. "I declare you do look like im. I heard im talk about you before."

She closes her window, and we go up the walkway and join em on the front porch where theres a davenport we can sit on. It looks like a pretty nice little house. I'm wonderin what Benjamin's story is, and Martin starts to tell it:

"Benjamin was married to the cutest little Indian gal yer ever gonna meet. Natchez Indian. Well, somethin snapped, and she just went crazy, so he finally committed her to an institution. They got a name for what she's got, but I be jiggered if I can remember what its called. He's been livin by himself ever since. Visits her once a month, but he says she dont hardly do nothin but sit and stare. He says she dont even know who he is. He's a streetcar conductor here in town.

He's always managed to keep his job no matter what this damn depression ever did."

The next-door neighbor comes walkin down her front steps carryin a tray with a coffee pot and some cups and sandwiches on it. That sure is a welcome sight for us. We're beat from all that walkin, and we're hungry, too. The sandwiches are peanut butter and jelly, and they sure do taste good. The lady next door (she introduced herself as Thelma Parkins) stays with us and serves us the food.

While we're eatin and enjoyin ourselves, Benjamin comes walkin up Third Street. You sure can tell him and Martin are brothers. They look so much alike they could be twins. He's dressed in the gray trousers you usually see streetcar conductors wearin, the ones with the black stripes down the sides a the legs. He's wearin a blue shirt with a charcoal colored sweater vest and a navy-blue conductors coat. His navy-blue hat with its shiny black beak rounds out his uniform. As he approaches, he gives us all a confused look, and when he recognizes his brother, he breaks into a wide grin and shakes his hand. After Martin introduces us to im, we all go into his house. Thelma Parkins follows us in and starts movin around the kitchen, preparing food. You can tell she's no stranger in this house.

After makin us feel at home, Benjamin disappears into his bedroom and gets outa his uniform as he's talkin to us thru the open door. He's askin after Martin's family. When he comes back out into the parlor, he walks over to a sideboard and takes out a long black chaw and bites off the end. Thelma brewed us a fresh pot a coffee and went back over to her own house. Martin and Benjamin talk like two brothers that aint seen each other for a long time. Benjamin goes into the bathroom every once in a while and spits a gooey brown wad into the toilet. The rest of us are just sittin around listenin. We're gonna stay the night. Martin and Quentin'll get the second bedroom, and the three of us'll sleep on the floor in the parlor. We'll probly have breakfast here, and then head out for the train yard in the mornin.

84

Ten

Once when me and Swede were in junior high, we played a softball game over at Logan Park. Our team was a ragtag bunch a kids from school that played against kids from other schools around North East. We had a coach that was a butcher in real life. We barely had nine players, and all of us took the streetcar over to the park on game day. It was the furthest away we had to go durin the whole season. We got off the streetcar in front a the park, and as we made our way to the ball diamond, we saw a bunch a hard lookin guys hangin around the bleachers, spittin in the dirt and actin tough. The other team was already out there takin infield. When they finished, we took our infield, and then the game started. A few people were sittin in the bleachers, mostly fathers a boys that were good ball players, men that maybe had hopes their sons might some day play in the big leagues, or even play for the Millers or the Saints. They was mostly rooting for their boys as they came to bat or when they made a play in the field. The rough lookin characters kept hangin around. They was our age.

We only played seven inning games, and around about the fourth inning, when it was our turn at bat, I left the dugout to get a drink from the fountain behind home plate. As I straightened up after I got my drink, I was facin one a the toughs. He kinda nudged against me and said,

"I'm gonna see yuh after the game. Unnerstand?"

I looked that chicken shit son-of-a-bitch straight in the eye and told im, "I'll be lookin for *you*, asshole."

He tried to push me, but I shoved right past im and went back to the dugout. My fuckin heart was poundin. From the bench I looked over my shoulder to see what him and his tough guy partners really looked like. Besides the one that chose me, there were three others. One of em was tall and thin, an Indian-lookin fella. They looked tough, but that dont makes no difference to me. I knew when I got done with that little shit, he wasnt gonna be lookin tough no more. We played the last three innings and lost the game. That was the first disappointment. The second one was when the coach broke me and the little prick up before I could give im a good ass-kickin, and with the help of a couple a those fathers that came to watch their kids play, he also broke up Swede and the tall, thin Indian-lookin kid. We all got on the streetcar without any more trouble and went home.

When we got off the streetcar back at school, we all went our separate ways. Me and Swede walked home together. We got to his house first. His big brother was sittin on the front porch with his girlfriend. When we told im what happened at the park, he said, "lets all three of us go back down there and look for em and take care of em." Swede's brother was bigger and tougher'n Swede. Plus, he was two years older and had some experience. So, he told his girlfriend to go on home, and then the three of us got on the streetcar back

86

down to Logan. When we got there, only a few people were around. Four kids were finishing up a game a over-the-line on the ball diamond. Twilight time. Goin across the field, we could see four people sittin in the bleachers. It was four kids, and two of em were the punk I didnt get a chance to deck earlier and the bigger Indian-lookin kid that chose Swede. As we got closer to em, they all four of em stood up, and you could see that if theyd had any place to go, they woulda run like hell, but there they was with no place to go, and us comin at em. Me and Swede walked right up to the two we was after. The other two scrambled down both sides a the bleachers and took off in opposite directions. Swede's brother just stood by and watched.

"I'm gonna kick yer fuckin ass," I said to the jerk that'd come up to me at the drinkin fountain. "You were such a bad ass before, lets see how tough you are now."

I grabbed im by the collar and pulled im down outa the bleachers. I only had to hit im twice, and he was on the ground beggin for mercy, so I let up on im. Swede did the same thing to the Indian kid. It was pathetic the way we made short work of em. I actually felt sorry for the poor bastards watchin em walk away from the park. I guess guys like that have homes and mothers that love em just like everybody else. Both of em's fuckin noses was bleeding, and they slunk away like whipped pups with their tails between their legs. And it wasnt nearly as bad as it coulda been. Swede's tough and he can take care of himself, but he's not mean, and he's not a bully. Me neither. The only reason we went back was cuz his big brother was so keen

87

on it. I dont think Swede woulda done it on his own. I mighta. When I think about it, the one word that best describes Swede is "gentle." As we got on our streetcar to go back home, Swede gave my shoulder a squeeze and said to me,

"I guess we got our revenge, huh, Antoine." My heart was beatin as hard as it was when I got back to the dugout after that other jerk chose me.

These thoughts and memories are on my mind as I lay awake here in Memphis, Tennessee waitin for the dawn and a ride deeper into the South. I dont know why I cant sleep. I'm plenty comfortable and tired, too. This floor aint soft, but at least its smooth, which is more'n I can say for any a the boxcar floors or any a the lumpy, sooty train yards I slept in so far. It aint the floor, and it aint the temperature that's keepin me awake. I think it must be forty-five, fifty degrees out-side, not really cold a-tall. I know what its like back home; its only two weeks till the first day a winter. And I dont think its the travelin that's keepin me awake neither. We been on the road over a week now, and I've got pretty comfortable with it by now.

I get up and step over Swede, grabbin my jacket as I move toward the front door. I'm goin for a walk around the block. Steppin out the door, I look over my shoulder to see that the house is completely silent. Everybody's sound asleep. I tiptoe across the porch and down the steps to the sidewalk. Its past mid-night and all of Third Street is quiet. I take a left on Third, and all of a sudden I realize theres this great big switichin yard on my right. We been sleepin right next to the damn train yard; I thought a couple a those whistles I heard before sounded close. Itll be easy gettin outa here. About a mile down the track an engine blows its whistle. I feel like its callin me. I finish my walk around the block.

Back at the house I climb the steps to the porch where I sit down on the old davenport and listen to the quiet Memphis night. Every so often a train whistle breaks the silence. All of a sudden sleep catches up with me and before I know what hit me, I'm out cold. I dont know how long I slept, but its still dark, and the chill a the night wakes me up. It aint freezin like back home, but its pretty cold out here, so I pull myself up and walk back into the house and take my place on the parlor floor where I fall asleep as soon as I put my head down.

Eleven

I'm sleepin pretty sound when I feel James and Swede stirrin next to me. James walks over to the window and is lookin out. I roll over lookin at his silhouette against the gray brightness of the first light a mornin which is comin thru the lace curtains. There aint a cloud in the sky, and right now the open space at the end a the street to the left a James is on fire with the risin mornin sun.

"Rosy-fingered dawn," James says while he's lookin at the red sunrise.

What a hell of a poetic way to describe it. That's exactly what it looks like. I dont say a word, and I'm not pushin im to explain nothin, but he turns around and looks at me, and I guess I got a question mark on my face, so he turns back to the window and explains what he just said.

"That's a line from an epic poem written a long time ago by a blind Greek poet named Homer. Actually, it was sung, probably accompanied by a lyre"

He's opened the curtains and starts to stretch and yawn in front a the window where an orange dome of sun pokes up over the horizon changin the color a the sky from deep, rusty red to pink. We're the only ones in the house that are awake.

"Say, James," Swede says. "Where'd you learn all that stuff anyways, and what the hell's a lyre?"

ANTOINE FAROT AND SWEDE

"That's a long story, Swede, but to make it short, I went to college for a while. University of Chicago back at the end of the war. I took some literature classes and that's where I read Homer. Its really fascinating stuff, and I oughta pass on some of what I know to you fellas. Since you kids arent in school, I could kinda make it part of your education. You could probably use some schooling anyway."

"Just when I thought we was all done with that," I say. "I wasnt never good at school stuff, so I dont know. Yuh think we could get it?"

"Depends on whether or not you like listening to my chatter, because all it takes is for me to tell you about it, and if we can find any books along the way, we can read them and then talk about them. All we can do is try. It really is fun."

"I'd like to pick up a mouth organ somewhere down the line, too, and you could teach me how to play it," I say cuz that's what I really wanna learn from im.

"On our way to the train yard, we could go back over to Beale Street," he says. "I saw a pawn shop that had some in the window."

We go out onto the front porch, which is now in full sunlight, and he starts tellin us some stories from what he calls the Greek myths. He starts out with some book called the *Iliad* which is the same book he pulled that quote from that was written by the blind guy. He tells us all about the Trojan war, the curse a the house of Atreus, the gold apple that Paris gave to Aphrodite. How Agamemnon sacrificed his daughter, Iphigenia, to soothe the goddess Artemis, and how Achilles got pissed off and wouldnt fight. Its a swell story. We

91

watched the sun rise and listened to im for over an hour. A little while after he starts tellin it, Martin and Quentin join us on the porch, and theyre listenin, too.

While he's tellin the story, Thelma comes out her front door wearin a coat and hat. She says good mornin to us and walks off down the street. When she comes back in about a half hour, she has a bag a groceries in one arm, and she dont go to her own house, but instead comes up the walk of Benjamin's house, steps around us and walks right in. James takes a break and stops tellin the story, and we follow her in.

She sets the bag down on the kitchen counter and goes back out the front door. All of us men start unpackin the groceries. She's bought a dozen eggs, some pork sausage, milk, cheese and cinnamon rolls. As we get it all lined up on the counter, she comes back wearin her apron and carryin some green onions and bell peppers.

"I harvested these from my garden. I'm gonna make you men the best omelets you ever had," she says. "Now, why dont y'all just go on into the parlor or dining room or some place outa the kitchen so's I can get started."

We walk out to the sun-drenched front porch. As the mornin moves along, we hear the train movement pickin up a couple blocks away. Whistles blowin, boxcars humpin.

"Doesnt sound like we'll have a whole lot of trouble finding some traffic out of here," James says offhandedly to no one in particular, but his eyes come to rest on Benjamin as he says the last word.

ANTOINE FAROT AND SWEDE

"I should think not," says Benjamin, spittin a brown wad over the rail into the flower bed. "Train yard's just over one block and down a block. If yuh dont see anything to yer likin there, you c'n go over a couple more blocks and theres some more, smaller switchin yards. Theres also the big yard a few blocks further south."

"Come an' git it," Thelma Parkins says, stickin her head out the front screen door.

We go in and take our seats at the dinin room table. After settin all the food on the table, Thelma sits down with us and leads us in grace. As we're eatin, James gets her to start talkin about herself. She tells us that she was born and raised right next door in the house she lives in. She never got married, and when her mother and father died, she inherited the house free and clear. She's been friends with Benjamin for twenty years, ever since he moved into this house.

"She was real helpful when I had to send Willow off to the sanitarium," Benjamin says. "They was best of friends. Why Thelma here goes with me when I visit her."

"Yes, she's a dear, sweet lady, and Benjamin and I miss her ever so much. It dont look like she's ever gonna get cured neither. She don't hardly recognize me and Benjamin when she sees us. Seems she dont recognize anybody. Just sits and stares. Lord willin, what happened to her never happens to me, or Benjamin neither."

"How about you, Martin?" James asks changin the subject, which I'm glad of cuz listenin to these

93

people talk about some screwball in the loony bin gives me the willies. "You gonna look for work right away?"

"I thought I'd go with Benjamin, see what the possibilities are for gettin a job with the streetcar company. Look into it anyway."

"I wouldnt get my hopes up there, if I was you," Benjamin says, "but its worth checkin on."

"Well, I'm just gonna go everywhere and put my name in," Quentin says. "There must be somethin in this town I can do and make some money doin' it."

"Golly, I hope yuh do," says Swede. "I'm sure if yuh look long and hard enough, yer bound to find somethin."

Swede can be so innocent sometimes. He looks so sincere as he's tellin Quentin, but what's he doin'? Gettin ready to be on the next freight outa town, that's what. Me too, and that's why I ain't sayin nothin. Course we'll be in Quentin's shoes when we get to California. We'll have to find work, too. But I have a feelin theres gonna be more opportunities for us out there than what he's got here. I always heard California's the land of opportunity. I'm just glad Swede's got an aunt out there we can hook up with. It gives us a goal.

We all finish our coffee, and James, me and Swede get our bedrolls together and get ready to walk on over to the train yards and check on the traffic goin south. When we're all gathered in the parlor, we shake hands with the Campbells and Thelma Parkins and head for the front door. When we reach the sidewalk, we turn around one last time and see the four of em standin on the front porch wavin to us.

94

ANTOINE FAROT AND SWEDE

I guess that's the last time we'll ever see em. Its almost like they dont exist, never existed, except in our memories. James says we should go back to Beale Street and pick me up a harmonica at one a them pawn shops that had harmonicas and saxophones and trumpets in the window, so we turn right on Third Street and walk the four blocks up to Beale Street. The first pawn shop we go into has a whole buncha Hohners, and theyre all in good condition, and theyre only a quarter apiece so I go ahead and pick out the one that looks like its in the best condition. I look to James and he says it's a good one. Then I fish a quarter outa my coat linin and give it to the pawn broker, and now I'm the proud owner of an almost new Hohner harmonica.

We head back down Third Street, and the first yard we come to is just a storage yard. No traffic there. We cross over Main Street, and theres a buncha sidings there. Theres a freight train crawlin along the thru track. Its only creepin along, so we get past the sidings and look up and down the track and dont see no yard bulls or anybody else. Just then theres an empty boxcar with its door open. As it passes, we trot alongside, throwin our bedrolls into it and hoppin on board behind em. We slide the door shut and go sit down, leanin against the back wall. We're all outa breath.

We only go about three or four city blocks and we're in the middle a this huge train yard. We're lucky we got on when and where we did. We got to pick our places in the car. Now fellas are climbin on like flies. We dont keep rollin straight thru this yard. Every so often, we come to a complete stop. When that happens, two or three men get on so that by the time we pull outa the yard, there aint much space to spread out. This is the fullest I ever seen a boxcar. Its funny how every one we hopped has been empty or maybe just had a few fellas in it, but not much freight. Maybe other cars on the trains have been carryin some cargo, but we always managed to get an empty one. Everybody in here seems pretty nice. I dont see Mousey or nobody that even looks like im anywhere. James settles back and plays his mouth organ, and I try my hand at mine tryin to go along with im on the melody. No sooner do we leave Memphis than a toothless old-timer next to me says out loud, like he was talkin to everyone in the boxcar:

"We done already passed into Mississippi, believe it or not. You ever been this far into the deep south, son?" This last to me.

"Nope," I say. I figure if I dont say no more to im, he'll think I'm smoother'n maybe I am.

"Well, yuh gotta watch out for these southern rednecks. They go around in white sheets and find colored boys and hang em from trees. And you dont never wanna get th'owed in the poky for nothin down here. They put you on the chain gang, and you like to never see yer home again."

"Wow!" Swede says. His mouth is wide open, and I see this fella's really got im scared.

"Course, a young white boy like you, with blond hair and blue eyes like you got, aint gonna have no trouble. You'll do okay."

Suddenly I'm hit by the realization that its only been a week since we left home. Last week at this time a day, we was just gettin ready for our Thanksgiv-

96

ing dinner. We've come so far and done so much in that short time that it seems a lot longer. Its been so long since I even thought about Ma or Sis or Wiktor Sadlo that they almost seem like those folks we left in Memphis. Did any of em ever exist? I'm wonderin.

Look at that! We just passed a train station with a big sign that says Winona. I walk over to the door and double check the sign as we rumble past. Sure enough, its Winona, just like back up in Minnesota. I bet its a lot warmer right now in this Winona than it is in that one. I go back to my place next to James and sit down. I dont think I ever felt so lonely at the same time I was with so many people. I mean, theres a good size crowd in here, and I feel so all alone. Even James and Swede seem like strangers to me now. Maybe cuz theres so many of us, it makes us seem unimportant.

Not a half hour outa Winona, the train slows down and some a the men scramble over to the doors to look out. Murmurs from those lookin out the doors are passed on to the rest of us: "Bulls!" So, we all get to our feet, and get ready to jump out. This time it aint so simple. There must be twenty-five men in this box-car, and we cant all jump at the same time, or we'd fall all over each other and maybe get hurt, so we get lined up by the doors, and get ready to move. A young boy I noticed earlier is standin next to me, almost pressed against me. He's with an older teenage boy, maybe nineteen or twenty years old. The kid himself dont look like he could be any older'n twelve or thirteen. After everybody was on, I noticed im cuz at first I thought Swede and me were the only kids here, but then I saw this other kid. So now he's standin between me and his

97

chum, and we're all waitin for the train to slow down enough so we can jump without gettin hurt.

All of a sudden the men closest to the door start leapin out. We must be gettin close to the bulls. As I get up to the door, I see theyre only a few feet away. I jump just as we get abreast of em. As I hit the ground, I ball up and take a real rough tumble down the embankment. My bedroll is tucked into my stomach; my arms're wrapped around it; I'm holdin on for dear life. At the bottom a the embankment, I get to my feet just as a bull is comin at me with his billy club raised above his head. He's big and clumsy and its easy to duck under his swing and get away from im. He loses his balance and falls over onto his back. The little kid's right next to me, so we scramble off into the bushes together. I dont see Swede or James or the kid's friend anywhere around, so the two of us huddle together tryin to be quiet. We're both shakin like a dog shittin peach stones and tryin to control our heavy breathin to be as quiet as we can be. Thru the bushes we can see the bull we gave the slip to lookin around for us, and he's cussin up a storm. Its at this very minute that I realize the kid aint a little boy, but a full-grown teenage girl. Scramblin to take cover, I ended up with my hand full on one a her tits. That's the way we are right now, and she is very slowly and silently movin my hand down to her waist, which I can also feel is a big-hipped girl's waist. Can you figure that? She aint pushin me away and is still huggin me tight, holdin on for dear life.

We can hear the cussin movin away back up toward the track. We stand up and we're all dazed and

98

confused and lookin for our friends. Plus, we're bruised and beat up from the fall from the train. Swede and James are together. The girl's friend is comin from the opposite direction. She sees im and runs to im. I join my pals and we walk off together toward the next town which we can see from where we are. We're between the railroad tracks and a creek that parallels em. The train has moved ahead on its trip south.

"Gee, I was hopin we'd make it thru here without havin to get off the train," says Swede. "I'm kinda scared after what that old man said back up the track there."

"Just keep walkin and mind yer own business and nothing's gonna happen," James says. "Besides, what did he say about being white? Nothing's gonna happen to us."

In spite of what James says, I'm alert and I start lookin all around us, expectin any minute to get jumped. Its the middle a the afternoon, and we actually have to take our jackets off cuz we're sweatin so hard. We enter this dusty little town that looks like it lost its way when it got to this century. It dont even have no paved streets. Theyre all dirt roads lined with rickety old houses that are fallin apart. The main street's only got one block with a plank sidewalk fronted by a general store and a hole-in-the-wall cafe. Its a pretty sad lookin sight. Amazin how much bad times we've seen since we left home. It kinda makes Minneapolis look good. And Minneapolis actually *is* good, except for the cold winters and Wiktor Sadlo.

We still got the thirteen dollars and twenty-five cents left from the five dollars we found in Milwaukee and the money we made movin the furniture. We head toward the general store. Thelma Parkins made us some sandwiches before we left Benjamin's house. All we need is somethin to drink with em. As we enter the store, theres three fellas sittin in chairs on the wooden sidewalk out front. Theyre all talkin in heavy drawls and chewin tobacco and spittin into the dusty road. They eye us like we're some kinda odd roadside attraction. Inside the store, the proprietor asks us where we're from, where we're goin and how long we expect to stay in town. He's just bein friendly and inquisitive. We get three bottles of pop, and then we walk across the street to a run-down little park, which is all overgrown with weeds and looks like nobody ever uses it. Theres a couple park benches, so we sit down at one of em and have our late lunch. This meal should tide us over until tomorrow. Its gettin close to sundown, and its actually so warm that crickets are singin their evenin song.

"Lets go south out of town and see if we can find us a place to sleep in the woods for the night," says James. "Maybe in the morning another train will be coming thru here and we can hop it."

We walk along the main street and outa town. The houses on this side a town are even more run down and grimy than the ones at the other end. Most a the people we see here are colored. I dont believe I've ever seen so many Negroes as I see around here. We keep walkin, James lookin straight ahead and movin pretty fast, me and Swede laggin behind and lookin open-mouthed at all this misery. James urges us on. Theres pine woods all around us, so when we get a little ways

100

outa town, we duck into em and find a small clearin where we set up camp. By now its completely dark out, so the first thing we do is build a fire. When we get settled around it, James takes out his mouth organ and starts playin the blues. I imagine from up in a tree lookin down, this must be a pretty peaceful scene.

Twelve

We're real tired and we start dozin off right away. I dont know how long we been sleepin, but when the commotion wakes us up, the fire is only a pile of red-hot coals with only small flames licking around em. We're hearin nervous, excited voices comin toward us from the road. About fifteen feet away from our fire in the darkness a the forest, we hear leaves rustlin around. From my position next to the fire, the sounds move from left to right and then retreat thru the trees. Its somebody runnin. I can still hear the excited voices approachin from the road. Then torches light up our corner a the pine forest, and theres five men standin in the middle of our little camp. They look like some a the bulls that've chased us off the trains we rode. One of em has a rope with a noose at one end, and a couple are carryin pick handles, the bull's weapon a choice. Two more, dressed in bed sheets and matchin white dunce caps, are carryin torches.

"You boys see a nigger boy come thru here?" one of em asks.

"No," James says. "But we heard some noise over that a way." He's pointin in the opposite direction the poor guy ran in.

"Over yonder?" the man says.

"That's right," says James. "That way," again pointin in the opposite direction. The five men go off the way he pointed. Their torches flicker off into the dark woods.

"We better get the hell outa here," James says as he starts gettin his stuff together real quick. "When those redneck assholes figure out that we sent em on a wild goose chase, theyre gonna wanna do to us what theyre trying to do to that poor colored fella theyre after."

We get our things together, throw some dirt on the remains a the fire and move off toward the road. We go left at the road and hurry along silently under the light a the moon, tryin to put as much distance between us and that lynchin party as we can. I sure hope that poor colored guy gets away. Our seein that little scene is almost like a prophesy fulfilled. Less than eight hours ago, some old man on a train told us about just such goins on, and then it happened. Swede's settin the pace for all three of us. He's in a real hurry to get the hell outa here.

"You doin' all right, Swede?" I ask. I'm doin' all I can to keep my voice from shakin.

"Yeah, I think so, but I wanna get the hell outa here quick as possible. I dont like it here, and its too bad, too, cuz this countryside is real pretty and the weather is real mild, but these white people are a buncha assholes. That poor bugger didnt have a chance against all those men. Fuckers sure are brave in a big gang like that, huh?" His voice *is* shakin.

"Yeah," James says. "Some people are just like that. What I dont understand is why white assholes like that hate black people so much."

We walk for another couple miles, and when we think we're a safe distance from that bunch a jerks, we cut back into the woods, find another clearin and pitch camp again. We dont build another fire, but instead we curl up and go to sleep after we catch our breath and calm down a bit. I aint got no idea what time it is, and I'm really too tired and scared to care.

The birds are already chirpin and its still dark out. The sky got cloudy durin the night. Its more like a real light fog than clouds, and its a lot colder now than it was yesterday and last night. We move real fast after we rub the cobwebs out of our eyes. We get our stuff together again and wrap up our bedrolls. Swede is ready to go; me and James are still rollin up our blankets. After we get everything together, we strike out for the road. The drab day breaks thru the trees as we head south down the road. We walk for about an hour without seein a soul, and then we come upon another town. Its still early, so there aint nobody out and about. The town's just now wakin up.

About a mile outa town, a horse and cart come up behind us. When he pulls up alongside us, the driver says,

"Y'all like a lift on up the road a spail?"

He's haulin a load a cotton bales in the cart. I aint never seen just-picked cotton up close like that; the only way I ever saw it was woven into a shirt or a pair a trousers or somethin. This is just big tufts of snowy white stuff. James climbs up on the buckboard next to the driver, and me and Swede climb up on the bales behind em. As we get movin, a stiff, chilly early winter breeze blasts us in the face. Its a good thing we all got

104

good coats. James says his double-breasted suit coat is amazingly warm when he pulls the lapels up around his neck. It aint heavy, but its wool, and its warm.

"Name's Luther Johnson," the driver says to James offerin im his right hand. James introduces himself first and then me and Swede. "Where y'all a headed?" he asks.

"Trying to get to New Orleans," James says. "Gonna head west from there. Destination's California. Been traveling mostly by rail, yuh know, hopping boxcars, but they got more bulls than you can shake a stick at. So, it isnt the fastest way to go, but we'll get there by and by."

"No doubt you will," Luther Johnson says. "I'm a goin as fur as Pickens mase'f. That's about five mile on down the road. You boys hear about the lynchin last night back up the road, near Durant? I heard they almost didnt ketch the nigger. Seems someone steered em off'n im, but not for long. They finally did ketch im. Its said they hung im. Poor devil. Folks say he made some kinda remark to a white girl and that's what got im in trouble. I dont know."

Ah shit! How rotten can it get? I look over Swede's way, and it looks like he's gonna start cryin. When I look at James, he's turned his back to me, and I cant see the look on his face so I got no idea what he might be thinkin, but I bet he's just as shook up as us. And this Luther Johnson here dont seem to be any different than those five men with torches and pick handles last night, but he does seem to have some sympathy for the colored guy we heard scramblin thru the woods. That does say somethin for im. I guess he really aint like them. I'm beginnin to think like Swede. I just wanna get the hell outa here.

The horse is cloppin along in the gray mornin. Swede and me are silent as Luther Johnson tells James how he was born and raised right here in the Mississippi Valley and aint never been outa here in his whole life, not even durin the war. The army wouldnt take im, he says, cuz he had flat feet, so he just helped his daddy sharecrop some land up outa Goodman.

"Fact is," he says, "I'm still on that same land. My daddy died five years ago. I jest stayed put, and I still do pretty good at it, depression and all. Hell fire, this here's my crop we're a haulin."

He seems like a nice enough fella, but what would he do if he knew we was the ones that sent the lynch mob the wrong way? Would he refuse to ride us any further, or would he even maybe turn us over to the lynch mob? Oh well, I aint about to find out by lettin im know. A train comes whistlin down the track and passes us at about thirty miles an hour. It slows down as it goes by. Then I notice the town straight ahead about a half mile. As we come up to it, we watch the train come to a complete stop just the other side a the town.

"Theyre fillin their water cars," Luther says. "They should be stopped here for over an hour."

"No kiddin?" says James. "How do you know?"

"It takes em at least that long to fill the two water tankers, and then they load some freight, cludin my cotton here, and they fool around a bit before they pull out."

ANTOINE FAROT AND SWEDE

"Well, it looks like we're in luck boys," James says over his shoulder to us. Then back to Luther: "You ever see any bulls around here?"

"Not to speak of. I seen em on the trains. They tend to stand out, but if you mean, do we have any hangin around the water tank? The answer is no. Least I aint never seen em."

This town aint no different'n any a the others we been thru since we got throwed off that last train. Its no more'n a dusty watering hole surrounded by cotton plantations and piney woods. You can tell just by lookin that the place has its own social order. The black people are at the bottom of it like they pretty much are everywhere, even up north. The people that live in the mansion with the Greek columns that we passed back up the road a couple miles must be the top dogs around here, and the Luther Johnsons are in the lower-middle. The different classes really seem to stand out, more'n back home. Seems that back home everybody's the same, poor. These differences are noticeable as we get to the center a this little town. The Negroes all walk out in the dirt of the street while all the whites are on the plank sidewalk. Theres one fella's dressed real nice, and all the men in overalls show him more respect than they do each other. He must be the one lives in the mansion.

Luther drives the buckboard over to a building next to the railroad tracks and parks it.

"Welp, this is the end a the line," he says. "I'm sellin my goods here, and then I'm a headin back home. I hope you boys get to where yer goin."

107

"We sure do appreciate the lift," James says. "It helped us a lot."

We climb down and walk over to the train and look things over. Theres five boxcars, some with cargo, some without. We dont see no bulls, so it looks like a pretty good bet. We wander around town for a little while tryin to not be noticed, tryin to fit in with the local folks, but the way we look, I dont think we do. Since we aint had nothin to eat yet, we go to a little lunch counter and order coffee and doughnuts. After each of us gets a cup a coffee and a doughnut, theres still thirteen dollars and seven cents left. We're really gettin a lota miles outa that first five bucks, and we still aint even touched the other ten. The man behind the counter tells us again all about the lynchin last night, somethin he didnt even have to mention, fars I'm concerned.

"Where y'all from?" he asks after he finishes tellin us about it.

"We started out way up north in Minnesota," James says. "We got outa there just in time to beat the falling snow. It sure is plenty warm down here, isnt it?"

"Sholy," he says. "Real warm in the summer, but not so warm this time a year. Where y'all headed?"

"Straight down to New Orleans and then west to California."

"Y'all gonna try to hitch a ride on this here train?"

"We're gonna try. Yuh got any suggestions?"

"Why sho," he says. "If'n y'all go on up ahead a the train a piece, yuh c'n duck inta the woods and wait for'm to get goin, and that's when y'all hop on.

108

ANTOINE FAROT AND SWEDE

Now dont go too fur, or the train'll be goin too fast for y'all to hop on. Dont try gettin on before she pulls out neither, or else theyll come and roust you off. Aint no bulls around here, but the other train men'll run you off sure, but they aint a gonna stop the train once they get rollin."

We finish our coffee and get ready to go look over the spot he told us about. We pay im the eighteen cents he charged us for the coffee and doughnuts and walk out the door. Its about ten oclock in the mornin, and this little burg is a very busy place. It looks like a lot a people just like Luther Johnson are bringin their goods here to be shipped south on the train. We might have some trouble findin room in one a these boxcars. We walk outa town, steerin clear a the train. We dont want the train men to get familiar with our faces. We get maybe fifty yards or so up ahead a the engine where the woods and underbrush are the thickest. We find a spot where nobody can see us, and then we just settle back and wait for the train whistle to blow. Thatll be our warnin that theyre gonna start rollin.

We're waitin maybe a half hour when, sure enough, the whistle blows and a great big cloud a smoke puffs outa the stack. The wheels start grindin on the track, and the engine gets closer to us. As it passes us, we can see the engineer lookin straight ahead, not lookin at us a-tall. The tender slides past, followed by the two tankers and then the boxcars. The train's still only goin about five miles an hour, but its gainin, so we jump out of our cover and hop on the first boxcar we can get the door open on, and we're rollin again.

Theres a couple hobos already on it. I guess some a this cotton is Luther's.

Thirteen

The trip thru the rest a Mississippi's pretty depressin. Its just a string a dumpy little towns and villages, except Jackson. That seems like a pretty good size town, smaller'n Minneapolis I'd say. We get off the train before it gets into town. The two fellas that were already in the boxcar when we got on told us they heard theres some pretty mean yard bulls in Jackson, frustrated deputy sheriffs that couldnt get jobs in that line. We took their word for it and jumped off when they did, which was when the train started slowin down just outside the yard. None of us got hurt and we gathered up our bedrolls and walked the rest a the way to the yard on the tracks and then cut over to the nearest road.

The yard's close to the middle a town, so we find a grocery store where we buy somethin to eat. We get some bread and milk, and the butcher cuts us some slices a ham and Swiss cheese. We wanna get some mustard and mayonnaise, too, but the glass jars they come in aint very practical for travelin (milk's bad enough, but we'll kill that off right now). Too bulky and too dangerous and messy if they was to get broke. And if you cant keep stuff like that cold, itll rot in a New York minute. We just take what we got and go back over to the southern end a the yard, check it for bulls, and then find us a comfortable spot under an oak tree where we make ham and Swiss cheese sandwiches and drink milk. All that's left when we finish are a half loaf a bread and a few slices a the ham and cheese.

Its around two oclock and we've just finished our lunch. We're waitin for another freight goin south outa the yard, and one's on the way. We can hear its whistle. And sure enough, here it comes around the bend. It dont stop at the station, but it does slow down enough for us to hop on, and we're on the road again.

The rickety Mississippi towns slide by, one exactly like the next, with tar paper shacks where Negroes live on the outskirts and run-down little houses toward the center a town where the color a the hunger and poverty is white. It aint real cold a-tall, but it wouldnt matter if it was, cuz we're in a car that's half filled with bales a cotton, so it'd be easy to arrange the bales so they keep us warm. The sun sits low in the sky. Its gonna be dark soon. James starts playin a tune on his harmonica. He tells us its a Jimmie Rodgers tune called "Brakeman's Blues." Says the song has some lyrics, and its really supposed to be played on a guitar, but since he dont have one, his harmonica version'll have to do. It sounds swell to me. Its so mournful and sad. I think about Ma and home and how far away I am, and it kinda scares me. What scares me more is not knowin if we're gonna pull thru this. When James finishes the tune, he tells me to take my harmonica out, and then he shows me how to play some riffs.

The towns slip past; the shingles posted at the little wood frame train stations say Hazelhurst, Bogue Chitto, Fernwood, Magnolia. Grand soundin names that seem tarnished now on such rundown signs. They sound like they should be carved in stone at the en-

112

trances of plantations. The afternoon is turnin to night as we get closer to New Orleans. The clouds are gatherin and almost as soon as we cross over into Louisiana, the rain starts to fall. We pull the door shut and huddle up next to the cotton bales. The rain drums on the steel roof a the boxcar. When it lets up and we open the door again, we're rollin along on a thin strip a land with two big lakes on both sides. Then we follow the shoreline a the lake on our left, and we seem to be bendin east. Its almost completely dark now, so its hard to tell which direction we're movin in. I see the lights of a city (New Orleans?) way across the water.

As we rumble along, the train moves away from the lake, and we pass thru another town, but cuz its so dark, I cant see a sign or anything that says what the name a the town is. After we go thru it, we curve up and move to within about a half mile a the lake again. Its black as ink and silent off to our left. I think its a lake. Could it be the Gulf of Mexico? I remember lookin at New Orleans on a United States map once in fifth grade. I was curious cuz it was at the opposite end a the Mississippi River from Minneapolis. Its near this great big sea called the Gulf of Mexico. Fact is, that's one a the spots the slave ships came in. I gotta get my bearings straight when the sun comes out tomorrow mornin. It still dont seem possible that winter's only two weeks away. The rains stopped and the weather's turned just like spring time back home.

We're startin to come into some population now. We're seein more houses on streets lit by street lamps. After we pass a cemetery, the train slows down, the blocks get shorter, and the houses are bunched close together. We must be in New Orleans now. When it looks like we're really in the thick of it, the train slows down even more. Warehouses and residential neighborhoods are all around us. It dont look like we're gonna have a welcoming committee of bulls here. The train just moves along toward the center a town. The yard's up ahead and not a bull in sight. We roll into the yard, and when the train stops, we jump off and start to walk toward the lights which we think is the right direction to get into town. Its still early, only about seven-thirty or eight oclock.

When we come outa the yard, we're on Julia Street. We walk to La Salle Street, and we cut over one block to Girod. I like all these French-sounding street names. We walk a few blocks and come to Saint Charles Avenue, and this is a real busy street with silent clickin trolley cars glidin up and down it. We take a left and go a few blocks to Canal Street. All of a sudden we're in the middle of a lota action. I dont know if I'd quite call it a party, but its somethin similar. On Bourbon Street Dixieland jazz blasts outa almost every joint on the street, and in some spots on the side streets, too. When we get to the corner a Bourbon and Saint Louis, I look down the street, and I'll be damned if theres not a joint called Antoine's. We walk over to take a look, and I see its a real swanky restaurant. A couple is just goin in the door when we get there, and we only get a short look inside as the door swings open and then closes behind em. Just inside the entryway I catch a quick glimpse of a chandelier givin off little blue gas flames. All I gotta say is it sure is swell havin the same name as a classy joint like this.

114

ANTOINE FAROT AND SWEDE

We go on back to Bourbon Street and walk past some more joints and hear plenty more music. Its a lot like Beale Street back in Memphis, except in Memphis the bands were more three-piece blues bands. Here theyre mostly five or more-piece jazz bands. Seems like inside every open door we pass, we see a banjo, piano, trumpet, saxophone, bass and drums playin some a the best music I ever heard in my life.

"That's some honest-to-God jazz, right there," James tells us.

I look at Swede and his face is all wonder and amazement, and he just stands there with his mouth open. So's mine, come to think of it. Its the funniest damn thing. To watch these people, you'd never think there was a depression goin on. Theyre all just havin a swell time. I dont think I've ever seen so many colored people in my life. But it dont bother me a bit. Theyre all havin such a good time, how could it bother anybody? This town looks so old. All these balconies with their wrought iron curlicues are sure somethin to see. From a little distance, they look like wire coat hangers all twisted up. We pass apartment houses with little courtyards in front enclosed by tall brick walls with black wrought iron gates standin open. Rickety old stairways climb to rickety old balconies with more curled wrought iron.

We only walk a couple blocks on Bourbon down to Conti Street where we turn right and walk down toward the river. At the river bank we take another right, and we're walkin toward a small carnival. When we get close to the first wagons and booths, I notice theyre lined up in two rows, makin a kinda midway. At the other end of it is a bigtop, but it aint really a big bigtop like Jim Bob Ray's was. We walk down the midway where theres all kinds of amusements: shootin galleries, pitchin booths where you try to knock metal bottles off a small round table with baseballs, and freak shows with a bearded lady and a man whose legs are like stone. The bearded lady's show is fronted by a cute little midget couple dressed in formal clothes, him with a top hat, tails and cane, her with a full dress like a weddin dress, except not white. Here it is the second week in December, and theres this carnival goin on with a lota people showin up just like it was the middle a summer. I'd never believe it if I wasnt seein it with my own eyes.

Movin along toward the bigtop, I catch sight of a gypsy wagon on my right. A heavy, dark woman with black hair sits in an open window with red velvety curtains pulled back watchin the people pass. Above the window is a sign that says, "Fortunes Told" in fancy letterin. In smaller letters at the bottom a the sign, it says, "Tarot Readings—Astrological Charts."

"Hey," I say. "Look at that. Tarot. That's like my name. Twice in the last hour I seen my name or somethin like it. You know what Tarot means, James?"

"Yeah," he says. "Its cards. Tarot cards. They have all different symbols and meanings, and gypsies are supposed to be able to tell your fortune from them. My ex-boss was a firm believer in them. He'd bring in a gypsy once a month just to read his cards."

"No kiddin?" I say. "I'd like to get it done. How much money we got left?" I reach into the pocket in my coat linin and take out all the money in there.

ANTOINE FAROT AND SWEDE

We're down to twelve dollars and eighty-seven cents. "I wanna find out how much it costs to get a readin."

I walk over to the wagon and go up to the lady. She's got long, danglin earrings hangin from her pierced ears. "How much for a Tarot readin?" I ask.

"Five cents," she says. "You want one?" I dont believe I've ever heard so soft and gentle a voice.

I walk back over to where James and Swede are waitin and ask em if they think we can afford it. I really wanna get it done, and both of em can see it, so they tell me to go ahead. Theres enough money for it. James tells me to give im all the money except the nickel its gonna cost me, and I walk back over to the gypsy lady. When I give her the nickel, she closes the velvet curtains and a shutter on the window, puts a sign out sayin she's busy, and invites me to step up into her wagon.

When I get inside, I'm struck by how quiet it is in there. Everything is maroon velvet with a lota fringes on the lampshades and over the door and windows. Right in the center of her little room, theres a round table about three feet in diameter with two chairs opposite each other. Theres a crystal ball and a small wooden box, just about big enough to hold a couple decks a cards, on the table. She offers me one a the chairs. When I sit down, I see a big circle drawn on the felt tablecloth. Looks like a pie divided up into twelve equal pie slices. Each slice has a little figure drawn in it: a bull, a crab, a couple fishes and a scorpion. The gypsy lady, whose name is Medea, tells me the circle on the tablecloth is the Zodiac. She removes the crystal ball and puts out all the lights except for one real dim

117

one that's hangin from the ceilin right above the table. She sits down in the other chair, and we are bathed in a pool of red light. The rest a the room is dark.

"Open your mind," she says to me. "Be holy of spirit." She's speakin so softly that I cant hardly hear her. Its so quiet; its like we're in another world. She moves the box over in front a her and opens it. The deck a cards inside is wrapped in navy blue silk. Its about twice the size of a regular deck a cards. Very softly and gently she takes em outa the silk and passes em to me. She tells me to shuffle em, and with my left hand, cut em twice so theres three stacks to my left.

"Select one of the groups," she says pointin to the three decks. I choose the middle deck. I almost feel like I'm in a trance, like maybe she's hypnotizin me. "Now, starting with the top card and the house of Aries, draw the cards one at a time and place them on each of the following houses going clockwise around the chart." She shows me the Aries symbol, the ram, which is twelve oclock for me lookin at the chart. I do what she tells me, and when theres a card on each of the houses (the pie slices) of the Zodiac, we both sit in silence for a couple minutes.

"Be pure of spirit and mind," she says softly. "Be open to the cards, for they will give you insight into your future."

She turns over the card in the Aries slice. Its the Fool. She tells me it means I will have many obstacles in my travels, but if I am aware of the knowledge that is contained in the handkerchief tied to the rod the Fool is carryin, I'll overcome these obstacles. She says this is a very good card cuz the Fool is the basis for the

118

very existence of the Tarot. She turns over the card on the Taurus slice. Its Death. I shudder as Wiktor Sadlo's image flashes in my mind. Medea tells me this card is not necessarily a negative thing. In death, there is re-birth, she says. The card on the Gemini slice is the Queen of Cups.

"See the sea shells in her crown?" Medea says. "They are symbols of the ocean and prosperous travel. You will be going to the ocean soon."

The card in the Cancer slice is the Hanged Man, which, she tells me, relates back to death. The Five of Cups is in the Leo slice. Medea says therell be some misfortune and disappointment that will bring on feelins a guilt. The Virgo slice is covered by the Six of Pentacles, which, Medea says, shows I have good money management skills and that someday I could be in a position to help others. She turns over the Seven of Swords on the Libra slice. She says this seems to con-tradict the Five of Cups earlier. Somethin about theft and greed.

"Perhaps these things will be inflicted upon you in the course of your travels," she says. "Keep a vigilant eye out for such activities."

She turns over the card in Scorpio, and her face goes dark. Its the Devil. She tells me I have to be vigilant against the Devil's temptations and try to find truth and the one goal. The card on Sagittarius is the Wheel of Fortune. Her face brightens up again, and she smiles at this one. She tells me its a symbol of the con-stant change in nature; therefore, she says, I gotta know that things are gonna change, so I better be aware a the past, cuz that's how I'm gonna know what to do when its my turn to fall off the wheel. Her smile gets broader as she turns over the Magician in Capricorn.

"This is good," she says. "Thru perseverance, industry, wit, and knowledge, you will achieve your goal. This knowledge combined with the Fool's knowledge will help you to overcome all adversity."

The card in the Aquarius slice is Judgment. She tells me that this one rounds out my fortune. Its the unity of man, woman and child on judgment day when they experience the last moments of conscious being. I'm not sure I know what it all means, but that's what she says. The last card in the Pisces slice is the Page of Cups. She tells me this one means that I'll master my talents. As she's readin this last card, the door opens and a dark young fella comes in. Medea and him dont acknowledge each other. He moves off to a darkened corner a the crowded little room and sits down in the only other chair in the place. Medea and I sit in silence for a couple more minutes, and then she stands up and moves to the door. I follow her and step down as she holds the door for me. As I'm walkin away, she scolds the dark young man for walkin in on us the way he did. James is waitin for me by himself.

"Where's Swede?" I say.

"He went to take a look at the rest of the carnival. How was it? You find out anything you didnt already know?"

"It was kinda fun, but I dont know how serious I should take any of it. Some of it was kinda scary. Like when I drew Death and the Devil. Her face got a real worried look when that happened, I'll tell yuh."

ANTOINE FAROT AND SWEDE

"How about the gypsy kid? What was that about?" he says.

"Nothin as far as I know. He just came in and sat down in the corner. It was all over by that time. Why?"

"That was why I wanted to hold the money. Here, put it back in your coat lining," he says, givin it back to me. "If you'd had any on you, he'd have taken it from you without your even knowing that he'd done it."

Gee, that's strange. I didnt think it was that kinda a place, which goes to show yuh never can tell. She seemed like too nice a lady to set me up to get robbed, but I guess James knows better. He aint steered us wrong yet. I'm real glad he's with us. We only walk a few feet further up the midway when here comes Swede, headin back in our direction.

"Anything worthwhile up that way?" James asks im.

"Theres a merry-go-round in the tent," Swede says. "The rest of its pretty much the same as what yer lookin at right now."

"Maybe we oughta see if we can find some place to sleep," James says. "Why dont we walk along the river a ways here and see what we can find."

We walk about a quarter mile further along the river when we come upon a hobo camp with a couple campfires burnin. We go over to the one with the smallest number a guys around it, and James asks one a the fellas if we can sit down with em. When we show em the leftover ham, Swiss and bread, they tell us to sit

121

right down. After we split it up among the three of em, theres still a little bit for us three.

We all eat what we have, and James picks up where he left off back in Memphis with the Greek mythology. He goes over what he's already told us and then he gets into the war: how Patroclus put on Achilles' armor and was mistaken for im and killed by Hector, how this pissed off Achilles and he went into battle and killed Hector, and how Odysseus thought up the wooden horse to get Greek troops into Troy. The six of us start to drop off one at a time, first the three hobos, and then the three of us. I'm the last one still listenin to James tell about the Trojan War. Then me and him drop off to sleep, too.

Fourteen

It never got more than slightly chilly thru the night. Maybe down in the high forties. We slept till dawn. The sun's just peakin over the eastern horizon castin a brilliant orange path across the river. I rub my eyes. Now that its daylight, I see where we just spent the night. It's a kinda sandy area behind the levee along the river bank. Its maybe a quarter mile or a little less from the water line up to the nearest house. We saw the lights in a row a houses last night; this mornin we see the houses. Theyre kinda run down little wooden cabins in a neighborhood that's mostly warehouses. I get to my feet, and, with the sun throwin its warm light on my head and chest, I walk down to the river and splash some water on my face. The chilly river water wakes me right up. It must be snowin back home and other places up river.

We roll up our bedrolls and start off back into town. The carnival is closed up and its pretty quiet and still over there. We dont have to worry too much about gettin some more money any time soon. We still got twelve bucks and change. I wonder what the chances are of us pickin up another five as easy as we did in Milwaukee. Walkin thru the streets of New Orleans at daybreak, I see how old a place it is. You can smell the age in things around here. Dont ask me to describe it, cuz I cant, but you recognize it as soon as you get one whiff. Its like that smell I remember when Ma used to take me and Megan to go visit old Aunt Rosie. Soon as we got in the front door and were surrounded by all that dark wood wainscoting in the entryway, I could smell the musty odor of old people in an old house. The air is like that here. We come to this place called Lafayette Square. I notice a hand bill tacked to a telephone pole on the corner. As we pass it, I see the word JOBS in great big letters.

"Hey, fellas," I say. "Wait up. Take a look at this."

We gather around the pole to read the handbill. It says somethin about cannery jobs at the Dumaine Street Wharf. An old man is walkin his dog around the square, so we go up to im and ask im where this Dumaine Street Wharf is. He gives us some simple directions. Just before we get to Dumaine Street, we pass by another square, Jackson Square, which is bordered by beautiful old buildings. One is an ancient lookin church with stalagmite spires reachin to the clouds. Its a Catholic church, Saint Louis Cathedral, and a mass is gettin out as we pass it. Not too many people come out, only enough to make us wanna cross the street and walk on the side Jackson Square is on. What a beautiful park it is! Its amazin how green everything is for this time a year, and palm trees, too.

When we turn right, theres a group a men gathered and blockin the street about a block and a half down. Just when we turn the corner, they start movin on down the street in a group. Some of em are wavin signs. We're almost a block away from em, so I cant make out what the signs say. The men are all in a commotion about somethin. Every so often, one of em shouts somethin out, a slogan or somethin like that. We just keep followin em down the street toward the river. All of a sudden they stop about three quarters a the way down the block. When we come up behind em, James taps one on the shoulder and asks im what's goin on.

"Strike against that there cannery right there," he says pointin at a metal building next to the river. "We're strikin for union representation. Theyre tryin to bring in scabs by postin hand bills all over town. We're gonna try to get a picket line in there and see if we cant keep the scabs from crossin it. We aim to shut em down."

When he hears that, James stops in his tracks and backs us away a little bit. I climb up onto the base of a lamp post, and I'm lookin past im over the heads a the strikers and I see a line a cops tryin to keep em away from the metal building. The cops are like a bunch a yard bulls, swaggerin up and down, wavin their billy clubs.

"Well, you can forget about that job," James says. "We're not gonna cross their picket line. If we do anything here, we'll support the strike by joining these men, but I really shouldnt even do that. There might be somebody takin pictures for the newspapers or something, and if I show up in a picture in the paper, I could be identified by certain people who might wanna get me in some hot water. We should just try to find work somewhere else. This is a good size town; maybe we can find something else."

So, we turn on our heels and take off. We go back up to Jackson Square where we sit down on a bench and try to figure out where to go from here. The more James drops these little hints about himself, the more curious I get about just who the hell he is and where he came from. I look at Swede to see if I can notice anything in his face that might tell me he's as curious as me. I dont see nothing there. I guess we're just gonna have to talk about it some-time. And what better time than now?

"Exactly what did you do before you went on the bum, James?" I ask all of a sudden.

To my surprise, Swede says, "Yeah. I'd like to hear the answer to that one." So, he's just as curious as me after all.

"Well, I suppose you boys do have a right to know something about me. I havent said anything be-cause I didnt wanna worry you with my problems, and I didnt want you to worry about there being any dan-ger. I'm really not a safe person to be with, but since theyre after me and not anybody who happens to be with me, I guess it isnt that dangerous for you boys. I do appreciate that you havent been too inquisitive about my past. Guess I should just come clean. Really, what do I have to hide anyway?

"I dont know where I came from. All I know is that I was on the street when I was a little younger than you boys. I was maybe thirteen years old when Car-mine Gallo took me off the street, brought me into his home and took care of me and raised me like a son. He had two sons of his own, and then there I was, James Morrison, in the middle. The older son, Pauly, went right into the family business when he turned eighteen and graduated from high school, and as the years

126

passed, he was groomed to take over for Carmine whenever he should retire. Mario and I were both sent to college. I eventually went to law school and became a legal counsel for Carmine and Pauly and all the family business, which was mainly bootleg whiskey.

"Everything was fine until twenty-nine when the stock market fell apart. Carmine had laundered a lot of his money in stock brokerages and in the market itself. When the bottom fell out, he lost about eighty percent of the family's wealth. By New Year of thirty, he and Pauly were both dead, fished outa the Missouri River one cold January morning. In fact, in a month itll be two years since all that happened. What a swell Christmas we had that year, huh? I dont know what happened to Mario, but I've been on the lam ever since I saw what happened to Carmine and Pauly. They were the only family I ever knew. I think, I hope, Mama's still alive. The Conigliero family moved in and took over the entire operation. I dont even know if theyre still lookin for me, or if they were ever lookin for me in the first place. Didnt think it was a good idea to stick around and find out. One reason I never got around to lookin up Lorraine out in Hollywood is I think somebody might be watching her, waiting for me to show up. You remember the furniture we moved to that river boat up in Cairo, Illinois? Well, the guy who owned the boat was Vito Di Napoli. His organization runs the rackets in Saint Louis and he's in cahoots with the Coniglieros who now run Kansas City. That's why I disappeared so quickly the other day. I didnt want him to see me. He wouldve recognized me. I figure if I just keep moving, theyll never catch me, if theyre even af-

127

ter me. So wha'da yuh think, boys? Now you know about me, you still wanna keep traveling with me?"

"Heck yeah," says Swede. "It dont matter none to me about yer past life."

"Me neither," I say. "Hell, I always thought runnin into you was one a the best things that ever happened to us. We'd be lost without you. And now yer teaching us literature, too. Dont know how we'd make it without you."

So now we know some about James's past, and I know why he wasnt talkin about it. It must be tough for im, losin half his family in such a gruesome way, and then bein on the run, always lookin over his shoulder, not knowin when somebody's gonna shoot im down, and worst of all, not knowin if the other half of his family is alive or dead.

"I kind of had it in mind that when we get out to California," he says, "you boys can try to get to Lorraine for me, tell her I'm in town, and I want to see her. Then maybe we can find out if anybody's watching her to get to me. Would you fellas be interested in doing that for me?"

"Sure," I say. "It'd be swell to go to Hollywood, see all them movie stars. And you can leave it to us to get in to see yer wife. Me and Swede know how to do stuff like that."

"Well, that's swell, fellas," he says. "Now what we gotta do is see if we can make some cash, or maybe we can get a meal in exchange for doin' an odd job. It wont be too long before we're gonna be getting hungry. Lets walk out into the neighborhoods and see

128

if we can find a house that needs some work done on it."

"We mi's well," I say. "We cant keep hangin around here. I'm startin to feel like a real third-class bum. If we're movin, at least we look busy, even if we're not doin' nothin but walkin."

So, we head back in the direction we came from. When we get back to Lafayette Square, we cut across the square so we end up on Saint Charles Avenue. We walk down this street watchin the streetcars pass us by. I'm half tempted to try to jump on the back a one like I used to do back home when I was sellin doughnuts, but I'm a little scared to try cuz now I'm a vagrant from outa town, and I dont know how the cops are around here feel about that kinda stuff.

We come to Lee Circle where theres a statue smack dab in the middle of it, General Robert E. Lee. We cut thru the circle and stay on Saint Charles. Now we're comin into some neighborhoods. Trouble is these neighborhoods are lookin pretty plush. These houses dont look like the kinda houses that would need odd jobs done around em. In fact, the people that live here must be so rich that they probly have a regular gardener and maintenance man to take care of any odd jobs that need doin'. At Washington Avenue all the houses to our left are these plush old mansions, so we go right on Washington and go up a few blocks to Magnolia. We make a left on Magnolia and on our left sits a house with tall grass goin to weeds all around it and a picket fence along the sidewalk.

"You boys wait here by the gate while I go talk to the owner of this one," James says.

Jerome Arthur

Me and Swede post ourselves at each side a the gate, and we watch James walk up the walkway to the front porch and rap the knocker on the front door. A lady answers the door wipin her hands on her apron. I cant hear what James is sayin to her or what she says back, but they carry on a conversation for quite a while. James steps aside and extends his left arm in our direction as tho he's presentin us. The lady gives us a nervous smile, and me and Swede smile back, tip our hats. Then, after talkin to her some more, James turns and waves us up to the porch. As we approach, she pushes the screen door open and lets us pass on into the parlor. She closes the front door and joins us in the parlor.

"Miss Dupre," James says, his hat in hand; me and Swede have taken ours off, too. "Allow me introduce my friends. This is Antoine and Swede. This is Miss Dupre, boys, and she's got maybe a couple days work for us around here. She cant pay us anything, but she can feed us and we can sleep on the veranda around the side of the house."

Three sides a the house have covered porches runnin their length. Its a very nice house; its just run down, in need of paintin and fixin. I guess that's what we'll be doin' the next couple days. Miss Dupre walks us thru the dinin room and kitchen to a service porch where she shows us some tools: hammer, saw, paint and some brushes. Then we go out the door to a shed that's out in the back yard. Theres some gardenin tools in the shed: an old lawn mower, a couple rakes, a shovel, a hoe, and a scythe. Next to the shed is a garden plot maybe ten feet by ten feet. Theres no crops in

130

it right now; theyve all been harvested. But its pretty clear just from lookin that this is the only part a the yard that she pays any attention to.

"With these tools, I think you can get that grass down to a manageable length," she says. "When you finish that, we can talk about doing some painting on the house."

After she goes back into the house, James takes the lawn mower, Swede takes the scythe, I grab a rake and we get busy. We're still workin at twelve-thirty when she calls us in for lunch. Swede's been usin the scythe to get the weeds short enough for James to mow em with the lawn mower, which is really old and dull so he has to keep goin over it to get it cut down. I'm followin em with the rake. One garbage can is full, and I'm startin to fill the other one. We're almost done with this job when we go into the house to eat.

"Are you French with a name like Antoine?" Miss Dupre asks me as we're sittin around the table havin lunchmeat sandwiches.

"Yes, ma'am," I say. "My last names Farot. My pops name is André."

"I thought so," she says, and is silent for a minute or two. Then she goes on, almost as if she's carryin on a different conversation with someone else, "Lot of French people in New Orleans. I'm French. My people originally came from Nova Scotia, up in Canada."

"I notice all the French names a streets around here," I say. "And they got that one part a town called the French Quarter, so I was figuring there was a lota French in this town."

131

"You know any French?"

"No, ma'am. My ma's Irish, so my folks never spoke it around the house, but Pop could speak it. I 'member when I was little, he used to talk in French when he was mad at Ma."

"When you were little? Did he get away from it as you got older?"

"My ma packed her bags and me and Sis and left im a couple years ago. I aint seen im in quite a while. I guess he'd still be cussin her in French if they was still together."

While me and her are talkin, I'm lookin at her more and more. She looks like she's older'n James, but probly not by much. She's a real good lookin doll under all that exhaustion and weariness. I bet she's a knockout all dressed up and wearin paint n powder. But such is life durin a depression. No time to look good. No money to spend on makeup. There aint even no money to spend on food. She seems to be doin' okay here, tho.

We finish our lunch and she hustles us outside and back to work. I finish rakin and sweepin the walkway. James and Swede dig up a scraper and wire brush from the service porch, and they go after the loose and chipped paint on the house. After I finish the last of the yard work, I find an eight-foot wooden ladder, and I take the broom to the eaves and upper walls which are thick with cobwebs and city soot. When I finish doin' that, I take a bucket a water and a scrub brush with a long handle and go up and down the ladder again scrubbin what I just swept. James and Swede are

132

workin right along with the scraper and wire brush gettin the loose paint off.

We work thru the afternoon doin' this, finishin just as the sun goes down and it gets dark. Now the place is ready for paint, which I guess we'll start on tomorrow. While we're puttin things away in the service porch, I can smell somethin good cookin in the kitchen. After we get everything put away, we go in there to wash up. A big pot a some kinda thick broth is cookin on the stove. It sure looks and smells good. I cant hardly wait till I get a taste of it. Miss Dupre is tendin to it and fixin some salad with vegetables from her garden. I been wonderin what she's been doin' in here all day while we was workin. Theres only so much housework here. The house dont look real different now than it did earlier when we was in here for lunch.

She tells us to go into the dinin room and wait until she finishes cookin dinner. Me and Swede sit down at the table, but James goes into the parlor where theres some books in a book case. He goes over to look at em. Skippin around on the shelf, he slides a book out here and there and leafs thru the pages.

"Take a look at this," he says walkin over to the dinin room table with one a the books. "*Ulysses* by James Joyce. Remember how I told you about the Trojan horse and how a guy named Odysseus thought it up? Well, Homer, the same poet who told the story about the Trojan War, told another story about Odysseus and his travels home after the war ends, and this is supposed to be that same story, only told in modern day Dublin, Ireland. Ulysses is the name the Romans

133

called the Greek warrior Odysseus. I'd recommend it to you fellas, but you really should start out with something easier."

Miss Dupre comes into the dinin room with the pot a soup and salads. She sets em down in the middle a the table, and James takes the book back to the parlor.

"You've got some interesting books in there," he says returning to the dinin room.

"I have a taste for good literature," she says. "I've read them all, too. Right now, I'm reading *The House of Mirth*. You ever read anything by Edith Wharton?"

"I read *The Age of Innocence*, when it first came out back in twenty," James says. "I was going to college then. I really havent read much lately, what with bein on the bum and all. I do like your selection."

Me and Swede are sittin there lookin and feelin pretty dumb listenin to em talk about all these books they read and we aint.

"This sure is good soup," Swede says. "What is it?"

"That's not soup, young man. Its filay gumbo. Its got chicken and spices in it, and okra from my garden. You probably noticed my garden out back. Theres nothing in it right now, but come spring, I'll put in some more crops. The garden is about the only thing I keep up around here. I have to. Sometimes my vegetables are the only thing I have to eat. Its amzing what kind of a meal you can make yourself with a little lettuce, tomatoes, squash and cucumbers."

134

ANTOINE FAROT AND SWEDE

"You seem to manage pretty well here," James says.

"Yes, I do," she says. "Fortunately, I own the house, so I've always got a roof over my head as long as I keep up the taxes."

We finish our dinner and me and Swede go into the parlor while James and Miss Dupre clear the table and go into the kitchen to do the dishes. I go over to the bookcase and pick up the book James was lookin at before. Its a thick book, so I turn to the last page and see its seven hundred and eighty-two. Then I notice that the last several pages dont have no punctuation. No commas or periods, just words strung together. I try readin some of it but its hard to read. Its boring, so I shut it and put it back on the shelf and walk away from the book case. Leavin Swede in the parlor, I go into the kitchen to see how James and Miss Dupre are doin'. By the time I get in there, theyre finishin up, so the three of us go back into the parlor and join Swede who has fell asleep on the davenport.

"Well it looks like its getting close to bed time, at least for Swede," Miss Dupre says. "Maybe we all should be thinking about getting some sleep. We've got lots to do tomorrow."

We collect our stuff, which has been piled up near the front door, and go out onto the side gallery to find a comfortable place to hit the hay.

Fifteen

I wake up in the middle a the night and find that James aint there. His bedroll's still there, all messed up, but he's gone. Swede is sound asleep. As quiet as I can, I slip outa underneath my army blanket and go down the walkway to the sidewalk. I'm thinkin maybe he got restless and couldnt sleep, so he went for a walk, but when I get out to the sidewalk and look up and down it, I dont see im anywhere. I go back into the yard and walk around the side towards the rear a the house. When I get to where Miss Dupre's room is, the window shade is glowin with light. Her room is in the rear corner a the house on the opposite side from where we're sleepin. She's got windows on the side and back wall. The back wall dont have no veranda, only steps and a small porch at the back door. I walk around back and get close to the rear window, and thru it I can hear muffled voices inside. I pull away and go back around to where Swede is still sleepin. I tiptoe up the steps to the gallery, go over to my bedroll, climb under my blanket and go back to sleep. This is the warmest I've ever been at night in December.

Next time I open my eyes, its dawn, fuzzy and gray. James is back under his blanket sound asleep. Swede's already awake and rollin up his bedroll.

"How long you been up?" I ask.

"Just a few minutes," he says. "I really slept sound. Cant hardly remember comin out here last night."

"You fell asleep on the davenport, and me and James woke you up to bring you out here, but you were kinda walkin in yer sleep comin out."

I stretch my arms out and yawn as I get out from under my blanket. Its another chilly but sunny mornin (warm compared to back home), and I can feel the coolness as soon as I get out from under the warm wool blanket. A thin mist a dew covers the freshly mowed grass. I get out from under my blanket and shuffle down the front steps and into the sun. On the walkway, where the first color a sunshine hits the top a my head, I turn and see Swede still foolin around with his bedroll.

"Hey, Swede," I say in a loud whisper. He turns and looks my way. "Com'ere," I say, givin im a nod and wavin im in my direction. When he joins me on the walkway, we go together toward the front gate.

"Yuh know he spent some time with her in her room last night," I tell im.

"I knew he was gone for a little while," he says. "I rolled over and didnt bump into im like I woulda if he was there. Course, I wasnt real awake, so I cant be too sure of anything, but I figured somethin might be goin on when he volunteered to wash the dishes with her."

"Well, I got up and walked around the yard lookin for im, and when I got to the back a the house where her room is, I seen a light and heard em talkin inside. It was actually kinda embarassin. I went right

137

back to my bedroll. Wha'da yuh think? Is she gonna let us stay in the other bedroom tonight?"

"That'd be real nice," Swede says. "Are we gonna be stayin here for a while?"

"I dont know," I say.

We turn around and head back up to the house to finish rollin up our bedrolls. James is still sleepin.

"Wanna go for a walk before he wakes up?" I ask Swede, noddin in James's direction.

"Sure. Might be a nice break before we start workin again. I bet she's gonna have us bust our asses again today."

Miss Dupre keeps a note pad and pencil in a little box next to the front door. I go over there and scratch out a short note to James and put it under the hunk a twine tied around my bedroll. Then I set the bedroll right next to his head so he cant miss it when he wakes up. Me and Swede go down the steps and out the gate. We walk back to Washington Avenue and head toward the river. The sun is gettin higher in front of us and to our left. When we cross Saint Charles Avenue, we come into this neighborhood (I think its the same neighborhood we was in yesterday before we went to Miss Dupre's house) of plush mansions on huge lots with carriage houses and guest bungalows. How can they live like that in these hard times? Sometimes I wonder.

We go a couple more blocks and we're at the river. Looks like theres a lota shippin goin on here. Couple blocks down on our left we can see a ferry tied up to a dock. Buncha people are lined up along the dock waitin to get on board. We take a right and go

138

about four blocks until we come upon these warehouses where, cuz its Sunday, nothin's happenin, but
you can see its a busy place durin workin hours, trucks
comin and goin, barges tied up along the docks. As
we're passin a gate in a chain link fence, some fella
wearin gray work pants, a brown leather jacket with a
fur collar, and a brown felt fedora comes up to us and
says he needs somebody to run an errand for im, and he
wants to know if we wanna do it.

"It probably wont take you but about an hour,
and you can earn a buck apiece," he says. "Wha'da yuh
say, fellas?"

"Sounds pretty good to me. Wha'da yuh think,
Swede?" I say.

"Where yuh want us to go, and wha'da yuh
want us to do?" he says in such a way that it sounds
like its settled and we're gonna do it.

"Yuh gotta go back down river to where the
ferry crosses. Yuh cant miss it. Mile or so is all. You'll
see a lota people waitin in line for the ferry. You've
gotta give a sealed envelope to the pilot. He'll give yuh
another envelope and when yuh bring it back here,
you'll get yer money."

"Well," Swede says. "Yuh better give us the
envelope so we can get goin. This is a rush job, right?"

"Okay, boys," the man says. "Follow me."

We follow im across the field of deserted
warehouses to a shed no bigger'n twelve by twelve. A
La Salle four-door sedan is parked beside it. Inside the
shed is a man wearin a suit and tie sittin behind a desk
with a telephone on it. Another fella, also in suit and
tie, is standin off to the side a few feet. We step inside

139

and stand next to the door while the fella we're with walks up to the guy at the desk.

"I found us a couple runners, Mister Levesque," he says. "Yuh got the envelope?"

Mister Levesque takes an envelope outa his breast pocket and hands it over to im.

"Yer on yer way fellas," he says, givin us the envelope. "Now dont get sidetracked. Go straight to the pilot of that ferry with this and bring back the one he gives yuh. We'll see yuh in a little while."

We leave the office and go straight to the ferry. It takes about twenty minutes door to door. We go into an office where the pilot is standin by a window that looks out on the river. He seems pretty impatient, and he lets us know he's been waitin, like it was our fault he had to wait. I hand over the envelope.

"Man, at the warehouse said you had an envelope for us to take back to im," I say.

He opens the envelope we brought to im and is readin the message. With his free hand, he reaches inside his coat pocket, takes out an envelope and hands it to me without lookin up or acknowledgin in any way that he did it. Me and Swede just turn around and head back to the shed at the warehouses. The La Salle is still parked next to it. Swede knocks on the door, and the fella that hired us opens up and tells us to come on in. I give im the envelope, which he immediately gives to Mister Levesque, and the other guy in the suit takes a roll of bills outa his pocket and peels off two aces and hands em to me and Swede. We're on our way out the door when the guy in the leather jacket tells us he might have another job for us.

140

ANTOINE FAROT AND SWEDE

"Check back with me at sunup tomorrow mornin," he says. "I'm expecting a big shipment of cotton to go outa here then. I'm gonna need some hands to load it. Thanks again for runnin this little errand today."

Well, that two bucks came almost as easy as the fin in Milwaukee. The only difference was we had to do a real easy job to earn it. We'll show up there tomorrow and load that cotton. Maybe we can get James a job, too. Get us enough dough to carry us all the way to the west coast.

We head back to Miss Dupre's house. It must be past nine oclock. James and Miss Dupre are probly up and about by now. When we get back to Magnolia Street, I notice that Miss Dupre's house dont stand out like it did yesterday with its tall weeds and messy yard. Now its all trimmed and neat like most a the other houses on the block. We go up the walkway to the front porch. The house looks deserted. Theres a note thumb-tacked to the front door. It says that they went to get some more paint and that we should start paintin with what there is out back. So, we walk around back where the paint and supplies are set out neatly on the back porch. They even left a screwdriver sittin on top a the can a paint so we can open it.

We're about halfway finished with the front wall a the house when James and Miss Dupre come back, each carryin two gallons a the same paint we're usin. They both look pretty tired. They must a had to go pretty far to get those four gallons a paint.

"We had to walk all the way over to the hardware store on Tulane Avenue to get this paint," Miss

Dupre says. "Its where I bought the paint youre using there. The store is closed Sundays, but the proprietor's wife is a good friend of mine, and their house is on the street behind their store. We went to the house, and I asked him to sell me some more paint even tho he was closed. He took us thru the house and we crossed the alley to the back door of the store. We've got enough here to keep us busy for at least a couple of days."

Well, how da yuh like that? What's she mean by "us"? So far she aint done nothin on this job. I wonder what the hell she does in the house all day long. Course I cant say I blame her for not wantin to do this job. It sure aint much fun. And today, just like she did yesterday, she disappears into the house while the three of us get busy with the paint.

"What's she do in there all day long?" I ask James quietly as we start paintin the side a the house.

"She's a writer," he says. "She's working on a novel right now. She's got a little garret set up in the attic with a typewriter and writing table. In her room theres a pull-down ladder along one wall. The dormer above the front porch is her garret window."

"Well, I be go to hell," Swede says. "I'd a never guessed she was doin' that. Although, I shoulda known with all the tapping on the typewriter, but it was so soft, I wasnt sure what it was. She must have that attic sound-proofed pretty good."

Me and Swede tell James about our adventure at the warehouse this mornin and how we should all be up pretty early tomorrow to get there in time for loadin those bales a cotton. Miss Dupre calls us in for lunch around one oclock. Since me and Swede aint had

142

nothin to eat all day, its a welcome meal, and since its Sunday and Miss Dupre probly aint gonna cook another meal after this one, its a full Sunday afternoon dinner. Good, too. Louisiana hot links and more vegetables from her garden, green beans cooked in a delicious creamy sauce. They dont go after it like me and Swede cuz they both had some breakfast while we was doin' our little job for the man at the warehouse.

When we finish eatin, we hang out around the dinner table talkin and jokin and havin a good time. Finally, Miss Dupre tells me and Swede to go out and clean up the paint stuff. We're gonna call it a day. Her and James are gonna do the dishes, and afterwards she says we're gonna continue the conversation we started around the dinner table.

"Maybe we'll talk some more about literature," she says. "James tells me he's been filling you in on the ancient Greek myths and epic poems. Well, maybe we can come forward a little. Talk about some more modern literature. I've even got some books I can give you that you might be interested in reading. You can take them with you on the trip west."

"We'd be obliged for that, ma'am," I say.

"Dont mention it," she says. "I've got an extra copy of a book by a fairly new southern writer named William Faulkner. I'll give it to James because I think it might be a little too deep for boys your age. It's called As I Lay Dying. It was published just last year. I've got a couple of others for you youngsters."

They go into the kitchen, and we go out and start pickin up the paint brushes and puttin away the paint. When we get it all put away, we go back into the

143

house and sit down at the dinin room table. James and Miss Dupre are puttin away the last dishes, and then they join us at the table. Before she sits down, Miss Dupre walks over to the bookcase in the parlor and takes out three books, the Faulkner one, The Adventures of Huckleberry Finn by Mark Twain, and The Sea-Wolf by Jack London. Settin the books in the middle a the table, she sits down and says,

"Here are the three books I promised you. These two should be pretty good reading for you boys."

"I know I'm gonna like reading the Faulkner one," James says. "I've never read anything by him, but I've heard about him. I heard he writes like James Joyce. Is that true?"

"Well, their writing styles are similar," says Miss Dupre. "Theyre both good with stream of consciousness, but their plots and characters are very different."

I'll be damned if I know what she's talkin about. It sure sounds educated to me, and James just carries on with her like he knows what she's sayin. I look over at Swede and he looks just as confused as me.

"Wha'da yuh mean 'stream a consciousness'?" I ask.

"Its a writing style where the author puts the reader in the mind of a character in the story and the reader follows that character's thought processes," Miss Dupre says. "The character may be thinking rationally or his thoughts may just ramble. *Huckleberry Finn* is kind of like that, but its more just straight first-person narration, where Huck is telling the story, but sometimes his thoughts ramble. You'll see when you read it."

"Boy," Swede says with a bewildered look on his face, "I never thought that tellin a simple story could be so complicated."

"It can be," Miss Dupre says. "But it doesnt necessarily have to be. Its only complicated if you try to over-analyze it. You can also enjoy a story for itself. The Twain book is a good example of that. Its a really good story all by itself."

"I can vouch for that," James says. "I read it, and it is a good story."

"I'm gonna start readin it right away," I say. "I remember when we was in Cairo, Illinois, and you mentioned how Huck and Jim were tryin to find it in the fog so's they could go up the Ohio River to freedom. It kinda sounds somethin like what we're doin'."

"You can even start tonight," Miss Dupre says. "Y'all will be sleeping in the house, so you can make that your bedtime reading."

It *is* startin to get late, and me and Swede are pretty tired from all the things we been doin' all day. Also, we wanna get to sleep so we can get up early enough to get that job in the mornin. Miss Dupre shows us to the other bedroom where theres twin beds with clean sheets. Me and Swede get into bed right away while she and James stay up talkin in the parlor.

"The man said we should be there by sunup," I tell James as he goes back out to the parlor, "so dont stay up too late."

145

"Dont worry," he says. "I'll be ready to go before daybreak."

Swede rolls over and goes to sleep right away while I prop my head up with a pillow and start readin The Adventures of Huckleberry Finn. I'm laughin by page five, and I'm asleep by page nine.

Sixteen

Its still dark when James shakes me awake from a sound sleep. When he's sure I'm awake, he moves over to the bed where Swede is and shakes im till he wakes up, too.

"Its five-thirty, boys," he says. "We better get moving if we're gonna get to those warehouses by sunup."

We roll outa the sack and I go to the kitchen and pump some cold water into the basin and splash it into my face. I walk back to the bedroom and put my shoes and socks on. When Swede goes down to the kitchen to wash his face, I fix my bed up, grab my jacket and join James in the parlor where he's ready and waitin to get goin. Swede meets us after a couple minutes, and the three of us are out the door.

We go down Louisiana Avenue to get to the river. When we first get on the street, its deserted, but by the time we get to Magazine Street, theres some signs that the city is wakin up and startin to move. Theres quite a bit a traffic and it seems like a lota people are goin in the same direction as us. We see a milk truck and an ice truck makin their mornin rounds. An old blind guy is openin his newsstand, rollin up canvas tarps and cuttin strings around bundles a newspapers and magazines. Its amazin how things roll along smoother when theres no weather to contend with. These people are movin along casually; it could be summer for all they care. The people doin' the same jobs back home are fightin blizzards and frost bite right now. Half the customers on the route aint gettin their milk or ice cuz the trucks are stuck in the snow. I wonder if it gets boring not seein the seasons change. Guess I'll find out soon enough.

When we get to the river, we take a right, and I see the warehouses we was at yesterday. We walk the five blocks or so down to Napoleon Avenue, and when we get to the gate we was at yesterday, theres a crowd a men millin around near it. Theres a smaller group a colored men standin off to one side. Course it dont matter what color any of us is. When it comes right down to it, we all got our hats in our hands. Its pathetic. I walk to the fence a little way from the gate where I can see in the yard. I'm lookin for the man with the leather jacket that sent us on the errand yesterday. There sure is a lot more goin on here today. They open the big double gates and all the men file into the yard and stand off to the side. Trucks loaded with cotton start pullin in. The man with the leather jacket shows up and tells everybody to line up. Then he goes down the line pickin men out.

"Well, I see you boys made it back," he says when he gets to me and Swede. "Told y'all I'd give yuh a job if yuh showed up, so just step right over there with those men." He's pointin to the group he's picked.

"Sir," I say before goin over there. "We brought our pal along. Could you take him on, too?"

"Why sho," he says, motioning James over with us. Then he turns to the remaining men and says,

ANTOINE FAROT AND SWEDE

"That's all for today. You men check back tomorrow. Maybe we can put you on then."

He didnt hire any a the colored men, and they slink away lookin downcast and unwanted. It fairly breaks my heart to see those fellas so rejected and beat down. All of a sudden I think about that poor colored guy that got lynched back up in Mississippi. Seems like it just dont pay to be colored down in this neck a the woods. It dont hardly pay to be colored back home neither. They was always gettin fucked over there, too. Only difference is down here theyre more open about it. Down here they got colored drinkin fountains, colored toilets, colored park benches. There it is. If yer colored, yuh got yer place. Up home it aint so open, but its there just the same. They got their neighborhoods, and we got ours; they got their schools and we got ours. Only difference is theyre not marked with signs.

The gray sky is gettin blue as the sun comes over the horizon. Twenty-five of us got jobs, and we all follow the man in the leather jacket over to a dock alongside the river. Theres a great big barge tied up there, and the trucks that came in the gate when we got here are all lined up along the dock, backed up to the barge. Theres five trucks, and he puts five men on each truck. These are big stake rigs. Bales a cotton are stacked maybe six feet high in em. Its about seven oclock and the foreman says we got till noon to get all the bales off the trucks and onto the barge. He sets us up so theres one man on the truck movin the bales to the tailgate, and then two teams of two carry em one at a time to the barge. Theres gangways at the front and back end a the barge. Its gonna be tough cuz we gotta

149

coordinate it so the guys carryin bales dont bump into each other and cut each other off. I'm the littlest one in our group so I get the job of workin on the truck. James and Swede are paired off with the other two fellas. One of em is a great big guy like Swede, and the other one is close to the same size as James. The balance makes it easier for em to carry the bales. I'll be damned if this work dont put us back to where we was in southern Illinois. The bales are about the same size as the bales a hay, but the cotton is much tougher on our hands than the hay was. After only an hour a this, my hands are pretty raw. Swede and James both have the same complaint. I dont remember the hay at Oscar's farm doin' that. I cant imagine people pickin and choppin this stuff all day everyday durin the harvest.

We get our truck unloaded by eleven-thirty, the second one to finish. The other three finish right behind us. Theyre paying us twenty-five cents an hour, so we end up gettin a buck and a quarter each for half a day's work. With the two bucks me and Swede made yesterday, that gives us five seventy-five in two days. Add that to what we got and its a grand total of eighteen sixty-two. A pretty good little nest egg to get us goin on our trip west. Now I'm startin to get anxious to get to California. I wanna see the California sunshine and the movie stars and the beaches. Our destination, Seal Beach, sounds like a quaint place. I'm curious to see what its like. I wonder if theres really seals on the beach or in the waters around there. How big a place is it? How far is it from Los Angeles and Hollywood? And I won-der what Swede's aunt's gonna say when we show up on her doorstep.

150

ANTOINE FAROT AND SWEDE

After we collect our pay, we go straight back to Miss Dupre's house. We should get there just in time for lunch. As we round the corner at Magnolia, I'm struck by how nice her place looks after only two days a cleanin and fixin up. Theres so much humidity around here that the lawn, which was brown right after we cut it two days ago, is already green. The little paintin we did has made a big improvement in the place. When we finish that job, itll be lookin real keen. Maybe then we can head west. Hop the earliest freight outa here goin to the coast. We probly should have a powwow to find out what everybodys thinkin. James might be plannin on stickin around here a little longer. Maybe Swede dont wanna go neither. I dont know for sure, but I think he feels about the same as me. He probly wants to head west, too. We go up the walkway to the front steps and up to the porch. Our boots make a pretty heavy sound on the porch, so before anybody can rap the knocker, Miss Dupre calls out her garret window to us. James steps back to the top step and leans back lookin up at her.

"Doors open. Go right on in," she says. "I'll meet y'all inside."

We go straight to the kitchen where she has some fixin's set out for lunch. We gather around the kitchen table. I dont hear Miss Dupre comin down her ladder. This seems to be as good a time as any to see how long James wants to stay here, so I ask im.

"We'll finish painting the house," he says, "and then we head west. Maybe day after tomorrow. How long's it gonna take us to finish? You tell me."

151

It sure is a relief to hear that. I feel like I should find out what Swede thinks, so I say,

"You ready to move on? I know I am."

"Yeah. I been ready since we got here, but that's okay. Its been fun bein here. Had some real good times, and we made some good dough, too. How much we got? Six somethin apiece? More'n I ever had back home. I'm ready for California now, land of opportunity. Lets go."

No sooner does he say the last word than Miss Dupre appears in the kitchen doorway.

"Did you boys enjoy your day in the cotton?" she says. She almost sounds sarcastic. And how does she know what we did all mornin? "Sort of gives you a sense of what its like doing slave labor, doesnt it?"

"That crossed my mind more'n once," I tell her in all honesty. "How'd you know we was workin with cotton?"

"What else would it be? You *are* in New Orleans, you know. Did you notice how the real slaves, the Negroes, cant get paying jobs like those you got today? Did any colored men get hired? I thought not," she says answerin my head shake.

"There were a lota white men who didnt get hired either," James says. "There were just too many guys for too few jobs. But you are right about the colored fellas. None of em got jobs."

"And they probably never will," she says. "Last hired, first fired. It becomes a way of life after so much repetition. As a woman, I can relate to black people's treatment as second-class citizens. In a lot of ways, women get the same kind of treatment."

152

ANTOINE FAROT AND SWEDE

I never have thought about it much, but the way she tells it makes me think about it in a completely different way than I ever thought about it before. Is there any truth to what she's sayin? It does seem like women dont get much credit for havin any brains. I know Ma was the brains in both a her marriages, yet she was the one that took all the abuse and insults. Talk about slave labor, that's the only kind she ever knew in marriage. I hope things are better for her with Wiktor now that I'm gone. I know that my bein there put a lota pressure on everybody in the house. I think that was cuz there was so much conflict between me and Wiktor. I still cant help thinkin the only way to make her life better would be to get Wiktor Sadlo out of it.

Miss Dupre fixes us lunch meat sandwiches, and she puts us right back to work paintin when we finish eatin em. So, the three of us spend the afternoon daydreamin out loud about sunny days on the beach in California, while at the same time we're paintin every outside surface of the house a plain, flat white. Miss Dupre clatters away on her typewriter upstairs. A little before sundown we put the lids back on the paint cans and clean the brushes. When we come in the house, Miss Dupre is workin at the stove gettin dinner ready. She's fryin a chicken and warmin up some greens. That's one thing she wasnt kiddin about. She said she'd feed us cuz she couldnt pay us. Well, she sure has done that. Every meal's been real swell. She's a good cook. I bet she could make a livin doin' it.

I dont remember much after dinner. We had a busy day, two jobs. The paint job will be finished to-morrow. I guess we'll also spend some time to-morrow scoutin out the train yard, see if we can find out about any traffic goin west. Right now, I cant hardly keep my eyes open. Me and Swede are two tired boys so we go straight from the table to the room we're stayin in and are asleep shortly after dark.

Seventeen

At last we're on the rails again. We seen plenty a bayous since we left New Orleans. The climate may be mild around here, but this aint nothin but a muggy damn swamp. A jungle. I seen enough weepin willows and other drippin-wet plants to last me the rest a my life. All they do is keep New Orleans dark on cloudless days. The gloom gets depressin, especially when the sun is out, and yuh cant see it. I'm glad we're outa there. I'm ready for some-thin different. I'm hopin Texas'll have some wide-open spaces, with skies openin out over yuh and not hangin down on top a yuh. We was only in that town five days, but now it feels like it was a lifetime ago, maybe cuz we did so much while we was there. It was only last Friday that I had my Tarot cards read, but now it seems so long ago that its like it was in another life.

We finished paintin the house yesterday around two in the afternoon. It looked swell. A little while after we cleaned up, we took a walk over to the same train yard we come into last week. After nosin around a little, we found out about this freight we're on right now. Its goin to Houston. That's a big city, bigger'n Minneapolis I bet. Oil town, James says. There should be lots a train traffic outa there. The way we're movin, we could get to the west coast before Christmas. Wouldnt that be swell? Christmas in sunny California. No snow.

Jerome Arthur

After we found out about this train, we went back to Miss Dupre's house and started gettin our stuff together. We was gonna be leavin early in the mornin, and we wanted to be ready when the time came. James and Miss Dupre were alone in her garret upstairs for quite a while when me and Swede were gettin our stuff together.

The floorboards were creakin overhead with their movin around. It sounded like one of em was pacin. I guess he was tellin her we was leavin. When I realized that this is what he was probly doin', I got a twinge a pain thinkin about Amelia back on the farm in Illinois. The way I snuck out was pretty rotten, but I really didnt have no choice. She wanted to come with us. Its easier for James to tell Miss Dupre without duckin out cuz she has her house here, and I wouldnt think she'd wanna leave it and her work to travel with us. But it seems James did have some kinda effect on her. When we was sayin our goodbyes a couple hours ago, she was cryin, and she said, "Thank you James Morrison for comin to me from wherever it was you came from." I bet she woulda come along if he'd asked, but he didnt, so we was outa there still a trio. It was a good stay for us. We got to eat and take baths every day, and Miss Dupre even washed our clothes for us.

We got on this train at nine oclock, and its still early in the day as we rumble thru swampy Louisiana. The mugginess takes all the fun outa havin warm weather. Its damn uncomfortable, not to mention dreary. I bet its real bad in the summer when the temperature gets real hot.

ANTOINE FAROT AND SWEDE

Theres a couple bindle stiffs in the boxcar with us. Theyre at one end; we're at the other. And sure enough, theres cotton on board, too. James plays some blues on his harmonica. I'm tryin, without much luck, to read some a this Huckleberry Finn. I can tell I'm gonna like the story once I get settled someplace and can read it. Right now, if I read anymore, I'm gonna get sick. Its the rockin and rollin motion. Besides, I'd really rather watch the countryside roll by, read the signs as we pass thru towns, doze off after a while. Sleepin's the one thing you can do in a boxcar and never get sick a doin' it. Its like goin back to bein a baby rockin in the cradle. Specially in warm weather. Swede's al-ready dozed off.

Finally, I fall asleep too. I have this dream about us bein in California, and me and Swede are standin at the corner a Hollywood and Vine. I dont know how we got there, but I know we're waitin for someone to come and tell us if James's wife is gonna come and see im. We're waitin and who comes along, but Jean Harlow. She gives us the message that Lorraine will be in a rear booth at the Brown Derby the next day at noon, and James should be there then if he wants to see her and talk to her. How strange dreams are sometimes. I mean, theres Harlow right in front of us, like she just walked off the set a some movie, The Public Enemy say, and gives us instructions on how James can have a meetin with his wife. She's very official, bein efficient like a good secretary, rather than the doll we all think we know she is. And the dream ends just when its feelin best. I'm all puffed up and proud that we arranged it so smoothly, and a course, its as

157

real as anything could be in dreams, and then I wake up and its over. I try to go back to sleep, see if maybe I can start dreamin the same dream, but its no use. I'm awake now and its over.

Its mid afternoon, and Swede says he thinks we're somewhere near the state line between Texas and Louisiana. Far as I can tell, the scenery aint changed a bit; it still looks pretty southern with more weepin willows drippin outa the sky. The sky even seems to hang up above like it was held up by the treetops. When I watch the countryside slide by, I'm reminded of the swell travel adventure this is. True, the circumstances aint the best, but I'm sure seein a lota different places and meetin some interestin people along the way. Its possible that I could get to every state in the country before I make it back home again. I already been in quite a few. Lets see, now. Minnesota's one, then Wisconsin, Illinois and Tennessee. Wait a minute. I missed one. We went thru a little part a Kentucky, then Tennessee, Mississippi and Louisiana, and now its Texas. That's eight. Only forty left to go.

About a mile outa town up ahead, we recognize the familiar sign a bulls. The train slows down for no apparent reason. I scramble over closer to the door, and when I look out, sure enough, there they are up ahead comin at us. Swede goes to the other side and tells us its clear over there, so we grab our bedrolls and are out the door in one move. We manage to get out and away untouched. As soon as the bulls are sure all the hobos are off the train, they get on board the caboose and the train disappears into the west. James's arm and Swede's wrist are all pretty much healed up,

158

but the wounds are still a bit tender. Its nice to escape without it happenin again. All us scattered hobos walk aimlessly in the general direction of the town up ahead hopin we'll catch another freight car from there.

We start hoofin it into the next town. Its a pleasant, sunny late fall afternoon. We go about another mile and a half, and cross over a river; a sign says its the Neches. Now we're in Beaumont, Texas. That's what the sign said at the edge a town. We're at the corner a College Street and Railroad Avenue, and we decide to go down Railroad. I dont know what we had in mind. James says somethin about maybe we'll find a train yard or maybe a track if we go this way, but I dont think so cuz the street veers away from the track we just got off of. If we needed to find the train yard, all we had to do was stay on the tracks and theyd take us right there. So, we go a few blocks down Railroad Avenue and we come upon a college. The sign on the lawn out front says Lamar College. A little further down, past the build-ings, some fellas are playin a game a touch football out on the field. We stop and watch em run a couple plays. A couple other fellas are runnin around the track.

"Aint it amazin how life just goes on?" I say out loud, but I'm only talkin to myself. "Here you have a bunch a college boys, playin football, takin girls out, probly gettin em drunk on moonshine whiskey, and generally havin an overall good time. I bet if you asked em about the depression, theyd say, 'What depression?'"

"Sometimes it doesnt seem fair, does it?" James says. "At least these fellas are going to college,

159

havin good clean fun. The ones who bother me are gangsters like that guy whose furniture we moved to the stern wheeler, Vito Di Napoli. Hell, he doesnt know theres a depression on either, but he's nothing but a murderer and a thief, stealing from working folks by extorting protection money from them. And I'm sad to say that I used to be involved with the likes of him."

"Well, I bet not all these fellas are sleepin in a bed a roses," Swede says. "They gotta study a lot, and they probly aint got much more money'n we got."

Old practical Swede comes thru again. Hell, I guess he cant even see that most a these fellas were born with a silver spoon in their mouth. What I dont get is where's it come from in these hard times? How do these fellas fathers make money when so many people aint got jobs? They must be makin a profit somehow.

"I bet there aint no more'n about one or two fellas out there that's strugglin with his studies or his finances," I say to Swede.

My show of scorn for em seems to intimidate Swede, and he dont say nothin more. We move off down the street leavin behind us the fall sound a some guys playin touch football.

We go back in the direction we came from cuttin off to the left, and we end up smack in the middle a downtown. After pokin around there for a while, we go over to the train yard keeping an eye out for freight traffic goin west. Almost all the other hobos that were rousted off that last train are hangin around the fringes a the yard. We move away from the yard, walkin across a vacant lot to where theres a couple old junk cars. James looks into the best lookin one a the two, a Packard sedan, but he backs away real quick. Someone's set up housekeeping in it. We walk over to the other one, a Dodge, and he looks it over real good and decides nobody's staked a claim to it, so we stake ours.

Its gettin late in the afternoon. We pretty much decide that we're gonna spend the night here and try to catch an early freight out tomorrow mornin. Me and Swede start gatherin some wood for a fire while James takes three dollars and sixty-two cents a the money and goes into town to buy somethin for us to eat. After we get the fire goin and while we're waitin for James to come back, I prop myself up in the back seat a the Dodge and try readin some more about Huck Finn. Huck's hidin on the island, scared to go back home cuz he dont wanna get beat up by his pap no more. He sure does do a pretty description of a thunder storm. As its gettin dark, I'm gettin ready to quit readin, and James comes back with the food. He takes a can a pork and beans, a loaf a bread and a quart a milk from a brown paper sack. He gives me two dollars and fifty-four cents change, and I put it with the rest a the dough. We heat the pork and beans in the can, and then we pass it around, each of us eatin right outa the can. We kill it off along with the quart a milk, and then we wrap up the last three-quarters of a loaf a bread to save for later.

After everything is secured, we sit around the fire listenin to James play his harmonica, and once again the sound, backed up by the near and distant train whistles, brings out a most melancholy and sad feelin

161

in me. Then I pick mine up and try to learn the riff. Swedes gettin sleepy, and so am I.

Eighteen

Like an alarm clock for some far away farmer, a rooster crows somewhere off in the distance. I open my eyes, and its still dark out, darker, it feels like, than when we fell asleep last night. I can hear Swede breathin real even up in the front seat. He's sound asleep. I shift my position, but it aint much use. This back seat's just plain uncomfortable. I lay awake for a few minutes, and then I go back to sleep. I dont open my eyes again until the gauzy light a dawn comes up on the eastern horizon. Across the field in the train yard, I see hobos movin around among the two trains lined up on the three tracks. They look like theyre jockeyin for position. I straighten up in the back seat a the Dodge and look over the back a the front seat to see that Swede just opened his eyes. He looks confused, like he's not sure where he is, but after scratchin his head and rubbin his eyes with his knuckles, he looks around and realizes he's in the same spot he was in when he went to sleep last night. James is still sleepin in his bedroll on the ground next to the fire, which is now just cold, gray ashes.

I get outa the car and stretch and yawn. The back seat of a car sure aint no comfortable place to sleep. I'm stiff all over from it. I never could stretch straight out, and I'm not that big. I can imagine how uncomfortable Swede musta been as big as he is. Both of us shoulda slept on the ground like James. It wasnt any more cold than in this damn car, and it stayed dry thru the night. Swede's right behind me outa the car. I get my bedroll outa the back and start rollin it up. James stirs under his blanket. When he sits up, I know the day has started.

We get our stuff together and walk across the lot to the train yard. Things are happenin here. Lotsa hobos hangin around. Soon as a train rolls out, theyll all be tryin to get on it, and I guess we'll be right there with em. I sure hope somethin happens soon. I dont wanna be stuck in this town too long. Its like a minia-ture version of New Orleans, drippin and overhangin. The difference is there aint as much goin on here as there was in New Orleans, but its still the same kinda swampy, muggy place.

We move off a little further down the line from the rest a the hobos. When one a the trains does pull out, itll be movin a little faster'n what we'd like by the time it gets to us, but by then we'll be the only ones tryin to get on, so we wont be fightin for elbow room when we do try to climb aboard. We're still in the yard; we're just at the outer fringes of it. We get back by some bushes, and while we're standin there not really paying attention to what's goin on back up where the other hobos are, we hear a commotion. I dont even get a chance to see what its about (loud voices yellin back up the line) before I'm swept up by James and Swede. The three of us are runnin and bein followed by the other hobos that are bein chased by about a half dozen yard bulls with billy clubs. We all make our escape outa the yard, but a couple fellas are complainin cuz they was a little too close when the chase started, and they got hit with the billy clubs. The bulls aint really swingin the clubs and crackin guys skulls open. Theyre more nudgin with the butt end, which hurts plenty, or usin the stick like a staff, grippin it at both ends to bruise arms, ribs, thighs and shins. Sometimes you get whacked across the upper arms and shoulders, like James back up in Illinois, but rarely right upside the head. Theyre dishin out just enough pain to make you think twice about hoppin freight cars, but we're all fairly driven to reach our destination, so we're willin to risk it.

Theres about a dozen of us hangin around, tryin to figure out how to get back into the yard without bein chased back out again. This is too far down the line for us to hop a freight when one does come thru. Itll be movin too fast. Right now, it looks like we're gonna be stuck here for a while.

"Why dont we just take a break," James says. "Lets take a walk around town and come back a little later. Its no use staying here. We'll just get frustrated when a train passes and we cant get on it."

That sounds like a real good idea, so the three of us move away from all those other frustrated hobos, leavin em to fret over whether theyre gonna get back into the yard. We walk into town where we find a drugstore on a busy street corner. We take three stools at the counter a the soda fountain. The place just opened up for the day, and the coffee is still perkin, so we have to wait for it to finish before we can get a cup. The wall behind the counter is one long mirror, maybe fifteen feet long, so we're lookin at our reflection while we wait. We look like a pretty rag tag outfit if yuh ask me. A sign is taped to the mirror just above the perkin coffee. Its stained and old-lookin, and its handwritten message says, "We reserve the right to refuse service to anyone." The proprietor is movin around gettin things ready for the day. He finishes what he's doin' at about the same time the coffee finishes perkin, so he comes over and pours us and himself a cup.

"Aint it a damn cryin shame that I gotta be doin' all this stuff mase'f?" he says to us as he fills the four cups. "Soda jerk was supposed to be here at eight oclock, and he aint showed up. No notice, no nothin. Just didnt show up. Pretty independent, I'd say. He's lucky to even have a job, times as hard as they are."

His complainin seems so pointless. He talks like he thinks his complaints might change the situation, but it dont look like anything like that's gonna happen. He takes his coffee and goes back to the prescriptions counter and fools around there for a while. Three men walk thru the front door and sit down at the opposite end a the counter.

"Say, Elmer," one of em shouts to the druggist behind the prescriptions counter. "Where's Jody?"

"Didnt show up this mornin," Elmer says.

"Well, I'll just get us three cups a coffee. That be okay with you?" the customer says.

"Sho 'nough, y'all he'p yuh se'f."

The customer walks around the counter, takes three cups from the open cupboard and fills em with coffee. He looks our way and says,

"Howdy, boys."

We all nod and say hello. He takes the three cups a coffee back around the counter to where the

166

other two are caught up in a discussion about politics and the president.

"I'm tellin yuh, these gall dang Republicans are gonna break this country. It started with Harding, and ol' cool Calvin kept it goin, and now Hoover's gonna break us sure. We gotta get a good Texas Democrat in the White House before anything's a gonna change."

"I dont b'lieve that'd make a rats ass bit a difference," the other says. "Its outa their control, Republicans and Democrats. Its in the hands a the rich. And they just keep gettin richer while we just a keep gettin poorer."

Same thing I heard Oscar say back up in Illinois. Seems to be the slogan of the depression.

And so, their conversation goes while we quietly drink our coffee. We're gettin off our stools and leavin, and theyre talkin about how corrupt the banks are and how it aint surprisin to see some a these bank robbers goin after em. As we're goin thru the door, theyre comparin these modern-day bank robbers to the old-time outlaws like Jesse James. Back on the street again, we head on over to the train line.

"Boy, everybody sure talks a lot about how bad times are, but nobody seems to be able to do anything about it," says James. "Not even the ones who have it in their power to do something to make them better."

"And who's that?" Swede says.

"Oh, you know, the politicians, the bankers. But they just cant seem to do it, or wont do it."

167

Jerome Arthur

When we get back to the outskirts a the train yard, most a the same fellas are still hangin around waitin for a train to move. Things are real quiet, and we didnt miss anything when we went into town. Its about nine oclock right now, and the weather looks like its takin a turn for the worse. The clouds are gatherin; it looks like it might even start rainin. When the sun goes down, it sure gets cold in a hurry, but compared to home its still pretty goddamn warm. It must be pretty close to sixty degrees. Back home I bet it aint half that, twenty, twenty-five degrees tops and probly snow on the ground to boot.

Up the line a way, the hobos are stirrin. Somethin's happenin. I can hear a train comin our way, and when I look up the track, I see one comin, sure enough. We move out closer to the track. The track bed is level with the ground right in here, so we dont have to worry none about runnin up a hill to hop on. Speed's the only thing we'll need to worry about. If it aint goin too fast, it should be pretty easy to climb aboard. But if its speedin up, we may not even try it. No use riskin yer life for a lousy ride on a freight train. Better to wait for the next one to come along, and one will, sooner or later. Well, here it comes and its building up a head a steam. A couple fellas manage to swing aboard, but that's about a hundred yards up the line. The engine is just passin us now. The engineer gives a blast with his whistle. Its goin pretty fast, and a few more hobos are runnin alongside, but only a couple more manage to get on. We dont even try. Its goin too fast.

The rain is startin to come down. We walk back over to the Dodge in the vacant lot. Nobody else

168

found it, so we go over and get in. Its fairly dry inside and we can watch the train activity in the yard from here. Sittin here watchin the rain come down, I feel cut off from the rest a the world. Now everybody has taken cover or moved indoors, so theres not a soul in sight and the only sound is the rain drumming on the roof a the car. Probly the worst part a this is the boredom. Nothin to do but watch the rain. This turns out to be a good time for me and James to do some readin, so we get our books out and start in. Swede's keepin his eye on the trains.

I'm readin the part about Huck's pap and how Huck came to the realization that he wasnt scared of im no more. That really hits home for me. Its kinda how it was on Thanksgiving when I realized I wasnt scared a the little Polack asshole no more. You just reach a point where yer tougher and quicker'n the little shit, and so you dont take his abuse no more. This Huck is really a funny kid, a laugh a minute. He finds humor in everything, no matter how sad the situation is. He laughs off everything.

"Hey, James," Swede says. "Take a look. Are those cars startin to roll?"

All three of us are squintin thru the rain, and theres a train rollin slow thru the station, and nobody to be seen, no bulls, and just a couple hobos. We grab our bedrolls and jump outa the car and are off on a run toward the slow movin train. We're gettin soaked, and muddy water is splashing up around our trouser cuffs. We cross over into the yard and run straight to the slow movin train. In one move I sling my bedroll onto a boxcar and jump in behind it. James and Swede are

169

right behind me. As we roll thru the yard, other fellas are climbin aboard. There aint a bull in sight. The weather must be too rough for em. Within minutes we're startin to pick up speed. It feels good to get clear a the yard and not see no bulls. We slide the doors half shut and then sit back wrapped in our blankets and watch the dark, rainy day slip past. Within the hour the rain lets up and the sun comes out.

After two and a half hours a dozin and readin, we roll into Houston, and as we come into the city, I'm struck by its bigness and its boomtown atmosphere. Its clear oil is the main thing around here, from the pumpin oil wells outside a town to the refineries and storage tanks closer in. The first yard we pull into is loaded with oil tankers. The train we're on is all boxcars, and we dont seem to be stoppin in this yard, but instead we creep thru at about ten or fifteen miles an hour. We eventually pass all the tankers and come into a bigger yard where theres more boxcars than anything else. Its here that our train pulls up on a siding and the engine cuts the boxcars free and moves off. We scramble down to the ground and go crunchin off thru the gravel of the yard lookin for another string a movin boxcars to get on.

About a quarter mile ahead and to our left, theres a bridge goin over the yard and the river that runs alongside it. Smoke rises from beneath the bridge. As we get closer, we see that its a good size hobo jungle. We walk toward it. As we walk in among the groups of men sittin around campfires, I'm recognizin some faces I seen in other yards and boxcars. All the campfires are under this huge bridge which is a pretty

170

good roof against the rain. It was comin down pretty heavy back in Beaumont, and then it quit for a while. Now its drizzlin.

We walk in among the campfires and James sees someone he knows. While me and Swede wait off to one side, he talks to a guy that's about his own age. He waves us over and introduces us to im. His name is Frankie and for some reason he reminds me of Joey, the mechanic we met back up in Jones-boro, Illinois. Now that we know a little more about where James came from and what his background is, I think I understand his friendship with fellas like Joey and Frankie. They was probly soldiers in mob families. We all sit down with Frankie's group, which is two other bindle stiffs.

Me and Swede aint sayin nothin. We're mainly just listenin to James and Frankie talkin old times and future prospects. After James tells im where we're headin and what our plans are, he says he's headed where we just came from, New Orleans. Somethin about a job with some gangster there that got his name from another mobster in Chicago. Its hard to understand what he's talkin about cuz he uses gangster lingo, but James seems to understand im pretty good. He tells James about a train that's gonna be leavin in the mornin for El Paso which is all the way on the other side a the state.

"The bulls aint bad around here a-tall," he says. "You can sack out right here tonight, and then you can cop a lift on that west bound freight tomorrow. I can guarantee you aint gonna get any heat around here."

171

Jerome Arthur

It is a nice place to be stayin. We're next to an abutment, so we're dry from one side and the top. Theres six of us around this huge fire. Its gonna be plenty warm. The smoky afternoon under the bridge drifts by and night falls. It gets dark real early this time a year. Its still a week and a half till the first day a winter, which is also the shortest day a the year. The sun sets real early that day, and then the days get longer after that. We stay at the camp, not goin into town cuz a the weather. It aint actually rainin, but theres a heavy drizzle. Just enough to get soaked if we go walkin into town, so we just stay put under the bridge. Not long after dark, I fall asleep. I dont know what time James and Swede dropped off.

Nineteen

The sun broke over the horizon a little while ago and then it disappeared into the clouds that drifted in behind it. We're on another train headin west. Its nice to be leavin Houston. Its too big. As we're rollin past downtown, I notice the Gulf and Shell signs on top a two tall buildings. Last night they was all lit up, and it looked like you could see em for miles around. A little distance past downtown, we hit the slums and warehouses, and then the neighborhoods. Finally the houses thin out until theyre on big lots bounded by gravel roads. Off to our right just as we're gettin into open country, theres this huge swamp. Now we're back on the open road again.

James says he thinks the next big town along the way is gonna be San Antonio. The countryside is beginnin to open up now, lookin more like the wide-open spaces I was expectin a Texas and the wild west. The colors have changed from swamp green to desert beige. Its easy to skip over the few small towns between Houston and San Antonio. This freight train barely even slows down as it whistles thru em. Not much is happenin. I prop my bedroll against the wall so I can get comfortable and get into my book. I cant believe how much I'm likin readin it. I never liked readin anything before, but I'm likin this. Its a good book. If nothin else, the story's entertainin as hell. Once yuh get used to his personality, Huck keeps yuh laughin yer ass off. He sure had a good idea killin himself off like he did. That way he was free to start a new life. That's what James shoulda done when he left. Now he's in this predicament. The people that are after im know he's alive. If they thought he was dead, they wouldnt be after im. But Huck didnt have no mom to worry about like I do. His pap was his only kin, and he was tryin to get as far away from im as he could. My ma would feel so bad if she thought I was dead. I'm sure she feels plenty bad enough after what I done to Wiktor.

James and Swede are both snoozin. Theres three fellas at the opposite end a the boxcar. This car aint got no freight so there's plenty a room to move around. My stomach's startin to talk to me. We was in such a hurry to get movin that we didnt get nothing to eat this mornin. I guess now we wont be eatin until we hit San Antone. Course if we get rousted sooner, we'll get somethin to eat wherever that is. In the meantime, I chew on a slice a bread from the loaf we picked up in Beaumont. Theres only a few slices left cuz we shared it with Frankie and the bindle stiffs at our camp fire last night. As I'm readin, I start to doze off, too, so I close the book and curl up next to James and Swede who're already asleep. I dont know how long I been asleep when I become aware a someone movin near me, hoverin over me. Without makin a move, I open my eyes to see one a the hobos from the other end a the boxcar rummagin around in James's bedroll which is right between me and him. When I realize what's goin on, I jump up quick and knock the bum down across

James's and Swede's legs, which wakes em up. Now all three of us have got the bastard pinned down.

"What the hell you wanna steal from me for?" James says. "I aint got nothin a no value."

One thing about James, he can use the right lingo dependin on who it is he's talkin to. He dont use "aint" when he's talkin to me and Swede. I never heard im use it when he talked to Miss Dupre. But he's usin it now, and he used it when he talked to Luther Johnson and the shopkeepers we talked to in the south.

"Sorry, brother," the hobo says, "but I was just lookin for a small scrap a food. I aint et nothin since yesterdee mornin, and I'm prit'near starved to death."

When he says this, I realize that he's just a bag a bones. With the three of us holdin im, he crumples.

"Well, we aint even got enough for ourselves. We're hungry, too," James tells im, and the three of us loosen our grip on im at the same time, and once freed, he scampers off to the opposite end a the boxcar where he came from.

James is pretty pissed off, and you cant blame im, but the poor hungry little hobo is so pathetic that you just got to let im go. He wasnt actin outa meanness. He was just hungry and was lookin for somethin to eat. Hell, I even done some scroungin around myself, if I ever got hungry enough. Yuh gotta give im somethin for havin the guts to come right in among us like he did to try to rob James. He musta known that with the three of us right there, he was bound to get caught. And he's damn lucky he tried to rob us and not some mean son of a bitch, like Mousey, that mighta thrown im off the train without even battin an eye.

175

"Yuh know," I say, "we still aint spent a whole hell of a lota this dough we got. Maybe we could spare im a dime or a quarter or somethin. Wha'da yuh think?"

"It'd be okay with me," Swede says. "Yuh can give im a couple slices a bread, too. We still got some, dont we?"

"Well, I dont know," James says. He's still got his doubts. "He did try to rob me. But I can see where he might've got pushed into it. I even boosted an apple or orange a time or two from the green grocer when I was on the street before I met Carmine Gallo. So, I know the spot he's in. And we may need our money later on. It may not seem like it now while we've got some, but later on a quarter may be the only thing we have. Oh, what the hell, I guess it'd be okay to give im a quarter. Maybe itll be enough for him to get somethin to eat in the next town and take away his need to try to rob somebody else."

So, I get out the last six slices a bread and walk over to his corner a the boxcar and squat down next to where he's sittin, propped up against a bale a hay. Him and the other two hobos are kinda cowerin away from me, like theyre scared I'm gonna start some shit with em, but I hold my hands up in the air which takes the heat off the situation.

"Me and the fellas decided to give yuh some of our bread and some money for somethin to eat next chance you get," I say, extendin my hand with the quarter held between my forefinger and middle finger. I'm holdin out the other hand with the six slices a bread. Timidly, he reaches out and takes the quarter.

176

ANTOINE FAROT AND SWEDE

One a the other two takes the bread. Then they thank me and quietly turn back into themselves. I go back over to where James and Swede are and sit down.

Its gettin on to noon time. I'd say its got a good ten degrees warmer in the last hour. It must be in the high sixties. Lookin out the door, I think I know why. We had a change a scenery. When I fell asleep, it was still kinda green. Now the countryside is like a desert, mostly flat with dry, tan-colored hills and huge rock formations here and there. Theres puffy white clouds in the sky, not rain clouds; its dry as a bone out there. It could be a scene from a Tom Mix movie. Its amazin how long we been travelin now without seein any bulls or bein rousted. Its actually so warm that we've got the door more than half open and we're not cold a-tall. We pass some cowboys punchin a small herd a cows. Dogs are yappin around the fringe a the herd, but we cant hear em or the cows cuz theyre so far away, and theres too much noise comin from the train. They disappear as quick as they appeared in the frame a the open door. The western scenery slips past just like it does in the movies, like its painted on a big scroll and someone backstage is crankin it from one spool to another. It sure is pretty, not like anything I've ever seen at the movies or anywhere else for that matter.

It must be about one oclock when we hit the outskirts a San Antonio. On our right is a huge wooden army stockade or somethin. It looks like it was probly an old fort in the wild west times. You can still see some a those old, rough-hewn wood buildings over there beyond what looks like barracks just in front of

177

us. We seem to be goin alongside it for quite a long time. Its big, whatever it is. As we pass it by, leavin it behind, the track bends to the left, and when I look out the door on that side, I see the tail end a the train movin at right angles toward us but fallin in line and followin us as soon as it hits the curve. Lookin out the other door, I see what looks like the downtown area maybe about a half mile off. The land here is so flat that you can see for miles. Theres mountains all around, but theyre so far away that they aint blockin no view. An adobe building that looks like its a hundred years old and a place with a sign on it that says "Menger Hotel" are on the edge a downtown. Could the adobe be one a the Spanish missions I heard about? I guess I'll find out if we stay here long enough.

We ride the boxcar all the way into the San Antonio yard, and dont get off until the train comes to a complete stop. We're real cautious as we scramble off the train, keepin our eyes peeled for bulls, but there aint none anywhere to be seen. We walk right outa the yard and into town. This town looks like its about the size a Minneapolis. We was on the road most a the day today, and movin at a pretty good clip, too, and I bet we're still not half way thru the state. But this town aint big compared to somethin like Houston. Its just that its a good size and its just another Texas town.

Our plan is to move on, not to spend any time here, but since all three of us are hungry, we decide to walk into town, grab a quick bite to eat, and head back to the yard right away to see if we can maybe make it to the next town before dark. We find a lunch counter a couple blocks away from the Southern Pacific Station.

178

ANTOINE FAROT AND SWEDE

James gets a tuna sandwich, and me and Swede both get hamburgers. James gets a cup a coffee; me and Swede get glasses a milk. We're probly not there more'n forty-five minutes. We eat our sandwiches and drink our milk and coffee, and then we head back to the yard. When we get there, we walk right thru the passenger area a the Southern Pacific Station. While we're there, James says he wants to use their toilet, so we go over to the men's room. James goes in, and me and Swede go around to the side of a shoe shine stand. An old gray-haired colored man is sittin in one a the chairs on the stand.

"You gentlemen like a shine?" he says to me and Swede as he lowers the newspaper he's readin.

"Oh, no thanks," I say, steppin back a step, tryin to hide my old scuffed and beat up boots. "But I would like to know one thing."

"Now what kine information you think I got, Son?" he says, foldin the newspaper up and puttin it on the seat next im.

He leans forward restin his left elbow on the top a his left thigh and his right fist on the other thigh. That way his face is closer and more on a level with mine.

"I was just wonderin what that adobe is out there next to the tracks before you come into the train yard."

"Why, Boy, dat's da Alamo. Its where dem white boys Davy Crockett and Jim Bowie got whupped by dat Mexican Santana. Dey got a plaque on de side a de buildin tells all about it."

179

Jerome Arthur

James comes outa the toilet so I thank the shoeshine man and we walk down to the southern end a the yard to find the best spot to hop a westbound freight. We still got three or four hours a daylight left, so we'll just go as far as we can until nightfall. We're movin west and we're startin to itch to get to California. We're talkin about it more, and all three of us feel it gettin closer.

After makin the necessary inquiries, James finds out that theres a freight goin to El Paso in about a half hour, so we find a comfortable spot where we can wait. Theres about four other fellas hangin around waitin, I guess, for the same train. I dont see the feeble little guy that tried to rob from James's bedroll. The last time I seen im was when we got off at the other end a the yard. I sure hope he found somethin to eat. Yuh gotta be in pretty bad shape to try to rob from someone that aint no better off than you. Poor people robbin poor people is just another example a how hard up we all are right now.

The freight train we want pulls out in a half hour. Its just like we had reservations and everything was on schedule. The afternoon is movin on, the clouds have cleared outa the sky, and we're on our way again, movin west across the dry, desert countryside. You can see for miles. Everything's so flat. The four fellas waitin in the yard are with us in this boxcar. None of em looks desperate enough to try to rob us, but just in case, we're gonna make sure our bedrolls are right next to us all the time.

Leavin San Antonio behind, we move out into open country. Its pretty desolate out here. Just like the

180

towns between Houston and San Antonio were hardly worth mentionin, so are the towns we went thru since we left San Antone. We roll thru em without takin notice, and by nightfall, after a beautiful orange sunset, the train stops in one of em, Del Rio. We're sure glad it stopped, too. As soon as the sun went down, it started gettin colder'n hell, and we damn sure didnt wanna be on a train goin forty or fifty miles an hour in forty-degree weather, and it feels like it might get that cold tonight.

So, we leave the yard and walk over into the downtown section. This is sure a nice town. Its a quaint little frontier town with a bank, a barber shop, a drugstore soda fountain downtown and wood frame houses in the neighborhoods. This is the first time I ever seen a lota Mexicans all in the same place. They sure look like they know how to have a good time. As the evenin turns to night, they seem to be the only ones out and about, havin fun in the restaurants and shops. Guitar music and singin are in the air. Its hard to believe that such a small town could be so lively, but then it is Friday night. It probly aint like this on other nights.

"Reason you see so many Mexicans," James says, "is because we're only a couple miles from the Mexican border. We'll see how it goes. Maybe we can cross over and have a look around. We'd be crossing the Rio Grande river."

As we're walkin around, we see a flophouse with a sign out advertisin rooms for a quarter a night. I'm thinkin it'd be nice to sleep in a bed tonight. The sign also says you can get a hot bath for a nickel. I look at James, and I guess he's thinkin the same thing I'm thinkin, cuz he says,

"How much money we got left? We got enough to get a room, you think?"

I'm the one with the dough in the pocket inside my coat linin, so I get it out and we count it. Theres seventeen dollars and twenty-nine cents.

"I dont know about you fellas," I say, "but I think it'd be nice to sleep in a bed. Been a few days since we slept in a bed, and we came a long way since then. We got enough dough for it."

They both wanna do it, too, so we go in and get two rooms next to each other with a door in between, one with two beds and another smaller one with just one bed. Its perfect. The bathtub is just down the hall. The whole works only costs us sixty-five cents. One thing's for sure, it aint the Ritz, but the sheets on the beds are clean, even tho the beds themselves aint. The curtains are threadbare, and the paint on the walls looks real dreary, but once the lights are out and we're asleep, we aint gonna see none a that anyway. I put my bedroll down on the pillow and take my shoes off and lay down. It aint the most comfortable bed I ever slept on, but its gonna do fine.

"Maybe we oughta go get us some Mexican food for dinner," James says.

"Boy, that sure sounds good to me," I say. "Should we start cleanin up right away?"

"I suppose. Its six oclock accordin to the clock down at the desk. Mexicans usually eat pretty late, so theres no rush, but we dont want to be too late. We probably should hit the sack fairly early. We want to check the traffic outa here as early as possible tomorrow."

I stay right where I am, relaxin on the bed, and Swede goes down the hall to wash up. James follows im after a few minutes, and when he comes back, I go. When we're all cleaned up and back at the rooms, we go downstairs and out to the street. We only have to walk two blocks before we find a Mexican restaurant. Its a swell restaurant. Theres a trio a guitar players walkin from table to table playin and singin a bunch a Mexican songs. What a swell time this is! We're the only ones in the place that aint Mexicans.

We get these huge dinners with beans and rice and enchiladas and tacos. Theres so much food we really cant eat it all, but we do. This may be our last meal for quite a while. We're stuffed, and it only costs us a buck and a quarter for all three dinners. After we pay the bill, I begin to realize that we gotta quit spendin so much money. At this rate, we'll be broke in no time. After dinner we walk back to the flophouse, and once there, Swede goes down the hall and runs a hot bath. When he finishes, James'll do the same. I'm gonna wait until tomorrow mornin be-fore I take mine. I start gettin undressed and gettin ready for bed. I prop my pillow against the steel top rail a the bed frame and start readin my book, but it dont last long. In a couple minutes I close my eye, and the book slips off my chest and drops to the floor, wakin me so that I move the pillow down, roll over onto my side and go to sleep.

183

Twenty

Travelin hundreds a miles in one day really takes it outa yuh. I was so wore out last night that I slept past sunup. I wake up and go down the hall and run some hot water. I soak in the tub for a few minutes, and then I wash up and go back to the room to get dressed. James and Swede are both rollin up their bed-rolls.

"We should probably scout out the train situation before we do anything," James says. "Find out if anything's goin to El Paso anytime soon. We may be stuck here for a while. This is a small town with a small yard, which means theres not gonna be much traffic. If we cant get out right away, maybe we can get across the border, see what Mexico's like. I've never been there myself. But of course, we'll want to get a train, the sooner the better. Isnt that right?"

"Yeah," Swede says. "I wanna be gettin to California, but if we gotta stay here for another day or two, we migh's well go have a look at Mexico."

When we find out that there aint no trains comin thru today, we cross over the border into a little Mexican village called Ciudad Acuña, just across the Rio Grande from Del Rio. It aint nothin but a dusty little one-horse town, and we're gonna spend the night here. We find a rustic little adobe-lookin cabin in a motel court for a quarter. We aint got no Mexican pesos, but the dueño is glad to take American money. We

shouldnt be spendin any more dough, but this is a deal
we just couldnt pass up for a quarter. And we gotta stay
someplace, cuz we found out the next freight train to El
Paso stops in Del Rio late tomorrow mornin.

So now we got a place to stay and right now is
siesta, and we're just relaxin, not doin' nothin. We're
sittin by the fountain on the patio separatin the two
rows of identical, stucco cabins with red tile roofs. Besides bein cheaper than that flophouse we stayed in last
night, this place is also cleaner and nicer than the flop,
but it is what some people might call rustic. I actually
feel like a half-ass big shot here, where last night that
place made me feel like a skid row bum. With its
stained, dark walls and sticky hall carpets, it just gave
me a sleazy feelin. It was noisy as hell, too. People
comin and goin all night long.

Not this place. So far we're the only ones
stayin here so we got the place to ourselves. We came
here after we walked down the main street around
noon. Everything was closed up, and the street was
deserted. We was the only people around. We was
lucky to even find the dueño here so we could rent a
cabin. Him and his wife were on their way to siesta
with her people when he stopped long enough to set us
up. This siesta stuff is swell. I see why its a big part a
every day livin what with the heat and all. If it gets into
the seventies this time a year, and I bet it must be at
least seventy right now, I can imagine how hot it must
get in summer. So wha'da yuh do in the middle a the
day when the sun's beatin down and you can't hardly
breathe, much less move around and work? You find
some shade and enjoy yer siesta. No need to find shade

185

today. The temperature's perfect for sittin in the sun. I wonder when they start movin around again, and then once they do, how late do they go to?

James gets up and goes into the cabin. Says he wants to take a nap. Swede picked up a copy a this week's Saturday Evening Post at a drugstore over in Del Rio. He's lookin thru it while I'm readin Huckleberry Finn. I'm not really concentratin on what I'm readin; instead, I'm thinkin about how quiet it is right now, which is okay for now, but I dont think I could live here and deal with it all the time. Its borin as hell. Its so slow that the highlight a the day is takin a nap like James. It crosses my mind that I could go for a walk, look the place over, see what its about, but then when I look around, what do I see? Not much. It'd probly take me about fifteen minutes to crisscross this pueblo, and that'd be it. I migh's well stay right where I'm at.

"So wha'da yuh think, Swede?" I say. "Nice setup we got here, huh?"

"Yeah. I like this warm weather. I wonder if California's like this. I wish we could get there pretty soon. This is okay, but I wanna get to California."

"Me too. And we will. We'll be outa here by noon tomorrow."

A new Model-A sedan pulls up in front a the court. Theres four men in it, and one of em gets out and walks over to the bungalow with the sign next to the door that says "Dueño." He's wearin a brown double breasted pinstriped suit and a brown felt, wide-brim fedora. Looks like he aint shaved in a couple days. After knockin on the manager's door and waitin and not gettin an answer, he walks over to us.

"Where's the guy runs this joint?" he asks.

"Dont know. Left right after he rented us this place," I say wavin my arm towards our cabin. "Town's pretty closed up right now. Dont know when they get movin again."

"You boys a bit young to be way down here in Mexico renting a motel all by yourselves?" he says.

"We aint all by ourselves," I say. "My big brother, James, is in the cabin sleepin. Swede here's our cousin, and the three of us are on our way to California where our Aunt Mabel lives. We're gonna live with her and get jobs."

"Jobs," he says sarcastically. "Aint no jobs in these hard times, not even out in the Golden State."

He walks back to the Model-A and leans in the window. He's talkin to one a the men in the back seat. After a short conversation, the one he's talkin to gets out and walks with im over to the cabin that's furthest away from ours. We're right next to the manager. Theyre goin to the cabin in back, in the opposite row from our place. The second guy's wearin nice pleated navy-blue trousers with suspenders, but no jacket. The sleeves of his white shirt are rolled up to below his elbows, and his neck tie is loose at the collar. He's also wearin a wide-brim fedora only his is navy blue. When they try the door a the cabin, it opens right up. None a the doors have locks. They both walk in, and after a couple minutes the one wearin the jacket comes back out and waves to the driver a the car to drive it on back and park it next to the cabin. I'm tryin to watch em

187

without them knowin I'm doin' it. When they get outa the car, the driver and the last fella in the back seat go to the trunk and take out two suitcases. After they disappear into the cabin, that's the last I see of em for the rest a the day. Swede's silent acceptance of my lie to the man in the suit tells me he knows why I did it and he woulda done the same. Who the hell is this guy with his three friends? He dont have to know nothin about us.

Me and Swede go into the cabin after a while. James is still nappin in the bedroom, and Swede joins im. Theres twin beds in the bedroom and a Murphy bed that folds outa the wall in the parlor. This little cabin is just like a house. Its more of a house than what I was livin in with Ma and Wiktor and Sis. Its better'n Swede's house, too. I get comfortable on the Murphy bed and start readin some more outa my book. The rate I'm goin, I might finish it by the time we reach the coast. I'm at the part where Huck and Jim just started floating down river on a raft they found, and theyre scared somebody's gonna spot em, and make em race to the Illinois side in the canoe.

While I'm readin, I hear voices across the way, so I get up and go to the window to see what's goin on. The manager has come back and discovered the new tenants. Apparently theres no problem as I see im turn around and go back to his cabin and go inside. So that's two cabins rented for the night. I wonder if anybody else'll come along.

No sound comes outa the bedroom; James and Swede are out cold. I go back to my book, and next thing I know, I'm fallin asleep, too. By the time I wake up, the sun has got down near the horizon, but its still plenty warm. James and Swede are at the table. James is playin a hand a solitaire, and Swede is still lookin at his Saturday Evening Post.

"It looks like we got some more tenants," James says. "A man and a woman. Swede tells me we've got four gents out in back on the other side."

"Yeah," I say sittin up. "We watched em move in. They come outa their place yet?"

"Not since I've been watching. I wonder what their game is. The man and woman seem to be fairly well off. Theyre dressed pretty nice, and a new Buick like he's driving there doesnt come cheap."

I get up and walk over to the window to have a look. It definitely is a swell lookin silver and red Buick four-door sedan with California license plates. Its got white walls all around and twin white wall spares in the front fenders with chrome mirrors mounted on top. That's a lotta car for just two people.

I take a chair at the table and watch James play out his hand a solitaire. Swede turns the page of his magazine. I start readin again. When the sun drops behind the horizon, James suggests we take a walk thru town to see what's happenin, so he puts his deck a cards away, and me and Swede close up our readin. Leavin the court, we notice that the two other occupied ones are all closed up like theres nobody in em. We go left at the first corner we come to and that takes us to the central plaza a the pueblo. Theres a fountain in the middle a the plaza, that has church on one side and a restaurant on the other. One little street that angles off from the plaza is lined with shops on both sides. This

189

was the street we walked down when we first came into town. Everything that was closed before is now open for business, and theres a few people out and about.

Not much is goin on. A couple old women come outa the church. The restaurant looks like it aint doin' much business. We walk down the street where the shops are. We find a store, "Tienda Morales," and go in lookin for somethin to take back to the bungalow to eat. Its real hard. Everything's written in Spanish, and the grocer dont speak no English. Up near the counter where you pay, theres a glass case with some sweet rolls. They look good, so we get three. The grocer calls em "pan dulce." He's a real nice, friendly fella. He knows we dont speak Spanish, so he goes outa his way to help us understand his. He holds up the sweet rolls with a smile and says, "Pan dulce." We repeat it, and he says, "Bien, bien." In the same case theres also a pan with some things that look like fried shavings of meat of some kind.

"What're these?" I say to the store owner, pointin at em.

"Chicharrones," he says with a smile. "Es puerco, muchacho. Entiendes?"

I'm sure he can see the question mark on my face so he holds up a picture of a pig.

"Oh, I get it," I say even tho I know he dont understand a word I'm sayin. "Puerco's pork, right?"

"Si, señor."

We go ahead and buy em along with our sweet rolls. Me and Swede each get soda pops, and James gets a Mexican beer. Aint no prohibition in Mexico.

190

ANTOINE FAROT AND SWEDE

We leave the tienda and walk all the way to the end a the street, lookin in the windows a some a the other shops, and then we head back to our place.

When we get there, the Model-A is gone, but not all four men went with it, cuz you can see someone movin around inside their cabin. The cabin where the couple's stayin is dark and silent. Their grand Buick is like a sentry guardin em in their sleep. We go inside our place and put our sweet rolls out on the table. We sit down and drink our drinks and eat our sweet rolls and pork rinds. Then we get ready to hit the sack.

After we get cleaned up, we hang around the table for a little while listenin to James play his mouth organ. The music sounds so good. Right now, it seems like my only link to the life I left behind. I'm a long way from home, about to fall asleep in a foreign country where I dont even speak the lang-uage, and somehow the music makes me feel con-nected. What could be more American than the mournful cowboy sound of a harmonica on a lonely desert night? I bet if we went outside and were quiet and listened hard, we'd hear the lonesome howl of a coyote. This is all so different from anything I'm used to. Minnesota's cold and wet; this is warm and dry. But when James plays a tune on his mouth organ, those differences seem to disappear, and everything comes together. When he finishes playin the last tune, he gives me a couple pointers on how to play. By the end of it, I'm playin a little bit.

Sometime in the night, while I'm sleepin real sound, I hear some noise from across the way. I get up and walk over to the window and look out. The Model-A is just pullin into its space next to the last cabin. Two

191

a the men get out and go back to the trunk, lift it up, and take somethin out. The lights are still on in their cabin. As they approach the front door, it swings open and one a the other men holds it while the two that just arrived carry their load into the cabin. The door closes behind em; the light stays on. I can hear James and Swede sleepin in the next room. I shuffle back over to my bed and go to sleep soon as my head hits the pillow.

Twenty-one

We never did make it outa here yesterday like we was thinkin the day before. We waited around the Del Rio yard from about nine in the mornin till about two in the afternoon and not a single freight train came thru. Only thing I can figure is they dont move freight on Sundays. The Southern Pacific passenger train came thru. The clerk in the drugstore where Swede got his magazine told us it was on schedule.

Even tho we shouldnt be spendin the dough, its good we're stayin inside. It gets a little too cold at night around here to be sleepin out under the stars. When we woke up in the mornin, there was a heavy frost on the ground. It got that cold overnight, but it warmed right up durin the day. Theres a thermometer over at the passenger platform, and I went over and checked it at around one-thirty and it was just under seventy degrees in the shade. So, we hung around and got warm in the sun, and by two oclock we decided to go across the border again and see if we could get our cabin for another night. By three oclock we was back in. Nobody new in any a the other cabins. Still only the four men in the back and the man and woman with the California Buick across from us.

The four men just hung around inside their cabin for most a the afternoon. From the look of it, they spent the whole mornin inside the cabin. A couple times one of em came out, got in the Model-A, and went somewhere. One a the times he came back with food; the other time it didnt look like he took anything out or brought anything back. Just went for a ride maybe.

I finally got my first look at the California couple when we went thru the plaza on our way back to the bungalows. They was drinkin wine in the shade a the outdoor patio at the restaurant, talkin about the surroundins, somethin about how the church and the plaza would be perfect for some scene. We was movin along, and I didnt really catch everything they said. They seemed like a pretty strange couple to me. He was an older, gray haired kinda stern-lookin gentleman. Debonair and cosmopolitan, but stern, too. She was young and beautiful, young enough to be his daughter, so beautiful that she coulda been a movie star. I took one more look at em over my shoulder as we passed. They talked pleasantly, enjoyin their conversation usin their arms to point out whatever it was they was talkin about. I seen em again after we was back in our cabin when they came strollin back from the plaza. She looked nice and easy with her arm looped thru his. He was smokin a pipe and gesturin with it. She'd look thoughtfully at the ground in front a her, either listenin to im or thinkin a somethin to say herself, and then she'd all of a sudden start talkin about whatever it was she'd just been concentratin on. The way she waved her free arm, you could see she was excited about whatever it was she was sayin, and she was havin a good time sayin it, too. They disappeared into their cabin, and that was the last I saw of em for the rest a the day.

ANTOINE FAROT AND SWEDE

*   *   *

The trip from Houston to Del Rio was long, and it wore us out plenty, but we sure got a lota time to rest up and get shut a the boxcar blues. All we did yesterday was hang around doin' nothin, which gave us a chance to get rested up. It was just like the day before on the porch at the cabin, only now it was in a quiet dusty Monday mornin train yard in Del Rio, Texas. We're all ready to get goin so I'm hopin theres a freight train that's just as ready. The sooner we get to California, the sooner we can get jobs, and I bet the opportunity out there is better'n here or back home; I dont care what that guy said the other day. I gotta believe theres somethin more there than where I came from. Maybe its wishful thinkin. One thing I know for sure is gonna be better in California, I wont have to worry none about seein Wiktor Sadlo every day and goin thru all the bullshit that goes along with im. For all I know I dont have to worry about im in Minneapolis neither, or anywhere else for that matter.

We're securin our bedrolls and gettin ready to get outa this joint again and get to the train yard. Its gettin on to nine oclock. We're all three rested up and ready to go, and I think for the rest a the trip we're gonna be out in a lota wide open space. James says if we get lucky, we could get to the coast in five days or so. That would put us there by Christmas. We get our bedrolls rolled up and tied, and we step outa the cabin and theres Virgilio, the dueño.

195

"Buen viaje," he says with a big smile. "Adios otra vez."

None of us is sure exactly what he's sayin. The only word we all recognize is "adios," so we say to im, "Gracias, adios."

As we're walkin away from im, I notice that neither one a the two cars is there, which dont really surprise me cuz I member hearin em both pull out, within fifteen minutes of each other, right around the time I was wakin up. Theyre nowhere in sight as we cross the plaza and head down the street where the shops are. We follow it till it takes us to the road that goes to Del Rio. We've come in off a Las Vacas Road and when we cross the river bridge it turns into Garfield. We're gettin close to downtown Del Rio when I see the Buick cross thru an intersection up ahead. We turn onto Main Street at a little after ten oclock, and we walk one block up to the corner a Broadway and Main. Up ahead in the next block, I see the Model-A pulled up to the curb. As we get closer, I see that only one a the men is in it, sittin at the wheel. The building he's parked in front of is a bank. He's lookin from side to side as if he's expectin someone to come along. Then when we get right up behind the car, the motor turns over and starts up, and a puff a smoke comes outa the exhaust pipe. We dont get more'n ten feet past it when the doors a the bank fly open and the three other men come runnin out with carpet bags in one hand and Tommy guns in the other. They hop in the car, and as it pulls away from the curb, one of em sprays the side a the bank with bullets.

196

ANTOINE FAROT AND SWEDE

We duck behind a parked car as soon as we see the guns, so we dont get hurt, but thirty seconds earlier we was right in the spot they shot up. As we get back to our feet on the sidewalk and watch the Model-A disappear down the street and outa town, we're surrounded by a crowd a people, the bank president, some a the bank's customers, other people that just happened to be there when it happened, and the California couple in the Buick. It was their car we ducked behind. They was inside the bank when the robbery happened. Everybody's followin the car with their eyes and not at all with their legs. They dont look too eager to chase after the robbers. A sheriff's car speeds by with its siren blarin.

"Lets get the hell outa here," James says in a voice that only me and Swede can hear, and then the three of us sorta back away from the small crowd. We duck down the first side street we come to and head straight to the train station. My heart is poundin as hard as it did the night those redneck crackers broke in on our camp back in Mississippi. Dont that just about cover it? I think I've seen it all now, a lynchin with grown men dressed in bed sheets and dunce caps, and a bank robbery where we was stayin in the same joint as the robbers.

We get to the passenger platform and walk down it toward the end a the yard. Before we get to where the thermometer is that I looked at yesterday, theres a bulletin board with passenger train schedules and a huge map a the United States with all the railroad lines all over the country. We stop and look at it for a while, tryin to figure out some distances and how long

197

itll take us to cover em. It looks like the next place we should try to spend the night is El Paso, Texas, then maybe Albuquerque, New Mexico or Phoenix, Arizona and then the next stop after that should be Los Angeles, California. Hell, it'd be possible to make it in just three days, but it aint likely we could move that fast, and it still gets too cold at night to do any travelin then. It dont look like its ever gonna warm up enough at night to ride the rails, not in a boxcar anyway. May-be a different time a year, like summer, it might be okay. Even tho we aint seen no bulls since Beaumont, we could get rousted, and that would screw up our progress in a hurry. And who knows, we might have to stop someplace and hustle up some more dough. The way we been spendin it the last couple days, if we dont get some more, we'll be broke by the time we get to the coast.

Accordin to this map and these schedules, a passenger train goes from Del Rio to El Paso in eight hours. We should be able to do better'n that on a freight train cuz they dont make the stops that a passenger train makes, but a freight train dont do the speeds a passenger train does, so maybe its a push, no difference in time. We could get there by sundown, but we'd have to be leavin pretty quick now. We'll be goin north again. I wonder if that means we'll be goin back into cold weather. We move off down the platform toward the yard.

"You fellas as outa breath as I am after that bank stick up?" I say.

"Yeah," Swede says. "My hearts still pound-in like a bastard. That was scary as hell. I aint never been so close to so much gunfire. Its loud."

198

ANTOINE FAROT AND SWEDE

"It was scary all right," James says. His voice aint shakin like Swede's. "But all that gunfire was just showing off. If we hadnt a ducked, I dont think theyd a shot us, but we did the right thing because you never know what somebody like that is likely to do. You know, I wondered about those guys when I first saw them. I didnt know what they were up to, but I had a feeling that whatever it was, it was no good. Just the way they dressed, they looked like hoodlums. And then the way they always stayed inside their place."

"And wha'da yuh make a that old geezer and his young lady friend bein right there when it happened?" I say. "Boy, its a good thing they was there. Their car was the only thing to hide behind."

"I wonder if theyll get caught," says Swede.

"Probably not," James says. "No doubt theyre someplace down in Mexico by now loaded with gringo cash. I imagine you could live pretty good down in Mexico with a small nest egg. Especially a nest egg of dollars and not pesos. If you had a lota cash, chances are you could live like a king. Look around you. It'd be easy to get lost in country like this."

A train just came thru the station and is slowin down in the yard. Theres ten cars besides the engine and tender. The first three after the tender are boxcars loaded high with alfalfa, and the last seven are loaded cattle cars followed by a caboose. Theyre doin' about ten miles an hour thru the yard when we swing aboard the last boxcar. As we continue to roll slowly thru the yard, we move some bales around so we have a nice little sheltered space where we'll be protected from the sound and the feel a the cold wind that always blows

199

thru a boxcar. After we get clear a the yard and get rollin into open country, James takes his harmonica outa his coat pocket and starts playin "California Here I Come." I try to follow along with im. I'm still not very good, but I'm gettin better. The music's a good boost, but we're gonna need more. We probly still got two more days a Texas. This is a big state.

After a while we get back into the lull a the boxcar rollin along the tracks. James's harmonica goes silent after about a half hour a steady playin. He starts readin the book that Miss Dupre gave im. Swede opens his magazine. I get as close to the open door as I can so I can watch the countryside go by. This part a Texas is a lot different'n the eastern part a the state. This is rocks and mountains, and the river cuts a green path right thru it. Not twenty minutes outa Del Rio, we start climbin thru a gorge and into the mountains, and then we're rollin right alongside the river for a few minutes. We climb to a ridge and theres canyons on both sides of us. I can feel us goin right a little and I see the river bendin left. And then it disappears from sight; who knows if we'll see it again? Now its all just mountains and desert and rock. As we keep on climbin, I notice that the sides a the mountains are all streaked with these jagged kinda furrows in different shades a red, maroon and beige.

"Hey, James," I say. "Take a look at this." He puts his book down and comes over next to me by the door.

"Those are striations," he says. "Theyre the scratches on the earth's surface that tell what happened here thru the ages. A geologist could come here and

200

tell you what it was like here a million years ago just by lookin at those grooves."

We're startin to get pretty high up before we level out. Mountain peaks rise up off in the distance. Now we're really in the middle a nowhere. We roll like this for a couple hours, and we come to a town called Sanderson. The train only slows down here and then hauls right on thru. As we're goin outa the town where the train tracks are close to the road right about where the two separate, we see the Model-A from Del Rio racin along the road, goin north and west just like us.

201

Twenty-two

Another couple hours go by and we're goin thru a mountain town called Alpine. This is the first greenery we've seen since whenever we last saw the river. Its been a steady uphill climb ever since Sanderson. You can actually see high mountain peaks with pine forests slanting up against em off to the north. Theres snow on the ground and its cold. We're in luck. The train dont stop in Alpine. It'd be nice if we go all the way to El Paso with no stops. It sure is a lot colder up in these mountains than it was back in Del Rio. As we whistle past another town without any kinda sign to tell us its name, I see this huge mountain peak off to our right about five miles or so. Its covered in snow. Right now, its pretty goddamn cold. I pull the door closed and go over and huddle with James and Swede. The weather out there aint real bad. As a matter a fact its sunny and clear, crystal clear and *cold*. We're freezin our asses off with the wind blowin thru the boxcar, and its gonna get colder, too cuz the sun has started movin down in the sky. I think we already saw the warmest part a the day about an hour ago.

The three of us get all wrapped up in our blankets, and when we huddle together, we can actually keep fairly warm. We dont go too far like this before we're all snoozin again. I dont know how long I slept, but when I wake up and go over and slide the door open and take a look, we're goin by another town. A big wooden water tank on top of a tower about a quarter mile off has the name Van Horn painted on it in great big letters. The sun moved closer to the southwestern horizon. I'd say we're about an hour from dark. No stop in Van Horn. The train banks to the left, and the late afternoon sun slants from the front thru the cracks in the left side a the boxcar. We come to a mountain pass at almost exactly the same time as the sun hits the western horizon. We go down into a river valley. The last a the day's sun is red as blood on the river's surface makin it look like lava flow or a snake on fire slithering outa the north.

By the time we reach the valley floor, the sky is a deep, dark blue. Itll be black in a few minutes. Therell probly be a moon like last night and the night before. There sure is a chill comin on with the night, but I think its warmer down here by the river than it was back up on that mountain. I'm sure glad we're not up there now. I bet we're still pretty high above sea level, tho. It keeps gettin darker and we keep movin further north, so I have a feelin that its just gonna get colder. I hope we're gettin close to someplace where this train's gonna stop. I been too cold for too long today, and I'm ready to quit movin.

We're rollin along close to the river for a few miles and then we move away from it. Pretty soon the lights of a town show up ahead. Its just a small town, but as soon as we pass thru it, we see the lights a the next town. They get brighter and theres more of em when we go from one town to the next, until finally we're rollin into what must be El Paso. These are the brightest lights we've seen since San Antonio. We

203

couldnt get here any too soon neither. I'm freezin. This aint nothin like Del Rio which was like a tropical paradise in comparison.

The train pulls into a pretty good size yard and comes to a stop. We jump off, and I think its already warmer just since we quit rollin, but its still plenty damn cold and gettin colder. We all three keep our blankets wrapped around our shoulders for a while after we get off the train. We walk outa the yard and roll our blankets up and start on our way into town.

"How much money's left?" James asks me. "If we've got enough, maybe we oughta think about getting a flop for one more night. Its colder'n hell, and I think the temperature is gonna drop even more in the night."

"Lets take a look," I say. Our breath comes out in big white clouds. With my frozen fingers, I fumble the money outa the hidden pocket in the linin a my jacket and count it out on a bench at a bus stop. Theres fourteen dollars and fifty cents. "Its gettin down there, but if we can find somethin for fifteen cents, a quarter tops, that'd be swell. We c'n afford that much."

It dont take much to convince Swede. It was a long, cold trip for all of us. He'd like to have a roof and a bed just like me and James. So, we go hikin off down the street lookin for a flophouse. Pretty soon we come to this rundown part a town. Ragged people are hangin around street corners, leanin against buildings, and hunkerin down in doorways drinkin from bottles in brown paper sacks, and some are lined up at a rescue mission. As we're walkin thru the neighborhood, we pass a dirty old two-story building with a storefront

204

ANTOINE FAROT AND SWEDE

hotel lobby. On the transom window above the front door, a sign done in fancy, but worn, old letters says, "Rooms." On the window a the door the two numbers tellin us its twenty cents a night are done in the same fancy, old worn out letters. We walk in and the man behind the desk, a great big fat guy with a green eye shade on his head and a cigarette danglin from his lips, gets off his stool and stands behind the desk waitin for us to walk up to im.

"How much for a room with three beds?" James asks.

"Well, I think it'd have to be at least thirty cents. I got a room with two beds in it already. We got a rollaway in storage. We can bring it on in. That'd be ten cents a bed."

"We'll take it," James says.

He fills out the register usin his own name. I dont think any a that's important, tho. From the looks a things around here, that little slip he just filled out will probly go right straight in the trash-can. Walkin down the hall to our room, we can see what kinda dive we're stayin in. The carpets are squishy. As we pass a pay telephone, I notice the wall all around it is covered with phone numbers and other little things people jotted down over the years. Each room door that we pass is all smudged and dirty around the doorknob. The gray walls have years of tobacco-smoke film and smudges where people with dirty clothes leaned up against em.

Our room's at the end a the hall next to the window out to the fire escape. That's good. If theres a fire, which looks like a good possibility in this place, we'll be close to a way out. We go into the room, and it

205

dont look bad for what it is. It's a good size with two single beds and a dresser along one wall. Theres a sink in one corner a the room. Under the window that looks out on the street, theres a radiator. It aint on, and the room is cold. As soon as he sets his bedroll down, James turns the knob down at the baseboard, and it starts ticking as it heats up. The flashin red neon sign of a pool hall across the street bounces off the opposite wall. James reaches up and pulls the shade down on the window. After a few minutes theres a knock at the door. When I go to open it, I'm facin a small hunch-back man with a black patch over his left eye.

"Here's the other bed you gents requested," he says, rollin his good eye up at me.

"Swell," I say. "Lets just roll it right in here."

We have to move one a the other beds a little and the dresser to make the rollaway fit. So now we're all set up for the night. Since we didnt eat anything all day long, we decide to find someplace close by and get a quick bite. The desk clerk recommends the diner in the next block. He says they got swell chili. We dont waste no time thinkin about goin anywhere else; we head right over there. Theres only one other person in the place, a man in rough-lookin, worn, threadbare clothes starin into his coffee cup and rollin a cigarette. We take three stools at the counter and look at the menu on the wall above the grill. The chili looks like a good choice to me. Swede and James say that's what they want, too, so we order up three bowls. Me and Swede each get a glass a milk and James gets a cup a coffee. It was a good choice. Its pipin hot, and its spiced up, too, so its really takin the chill out of us. Its

206

good, too, just like the desk clerk said, and we each get a slice of whole wheat bread with it. We hang around in there for a little while after we finish eatin. A couple more late-night diners and coffee drinkers straggle in. Its nine-thirty by the clock behind the counter when we pay the check at the cash register. All that good food only cost us forty cents.

We go right straight back to the flophouse and hit the sack right away. I end up on the rollaway, and boy is it uncomfortable, not much better'n the Chevy in Jonesboro or the Dodge in Beaumont. The other beds, with their steel head frames, dont look very comfortable neither. In the mornin I'll have to ask the boys how they were. What we got is a whole hell of a lot better'n what we'd have if we was out on the street. The room got nice and warm while we was eatin. Pullin down the shade did two things at once: it kept the heat in and the flashing red neon out. Just to make sure I dont get cold in the night, I throw my own wool blanket over the hotel bedding. I prop my pillow up against the wall, and I get set up to read my book.

James is tellin us that if we get the right breaks, we could be out in California by the weekend, or maybe even sooner. That's about the best news Swede would wanna get right now. He's anxious to get to his aunts house. I think he wants to get in touch with his family back home, just to let em know he's okay. I aint really thought much about stuff like that, and I know I should. I'm gonna have to find out for sure what happened to Wiktor, and I know I gotta touch base with Ma so she'll know I'm okay. Once I get those two things outa the way, then maybe I can start livin my new life in California. Get a job and find someplace to live, maybe on the beach. Its somethin to shoot for anyway.

As we start homin in on our goal, James is startin to show more interest in gettin there, too. The possibility of seein his wife is makin im nervous, so, like Swede, he's gettin anxious about gettin there. You can see both of em full a hope as they try to go to sleep and cant. I read Huck's story, the parts where he loses the raft in the fog and how he finds it again, and then how him and Jim run right by Cairo cuz of the heavy fog. When he swims ashore in Arkansas and takes the alias George Jackson, I start to drop off, so I close the book and pull the covers up and go to sleep.

Twenty-three

I wake up a little before dawn and lay there for a few minutes before I notice the red neon aint blinkin on the other side a the shade. I get up outa bed and walk over to the window and let the shade up enough so I can look out. The only light out there at this hour comes from the street lamp down on the corner. The pool hall is closed and all its lights are out. I see the frosty white roof of a house across the street and a block over. As I look straight down at the street below, theres three cars parked there. They all have a thin film a frost on their roofs, hoods and windshields. It almost looks like it does back home after an overnight snowfall, but you can see that this is just a slight dustin and will probly be gone as soon as the sun comes up. I get a chill just lookin out the window. I'm sure glad we got this radiator to keep us warm.

I pull the shade down and walk back over to my bed. I crawl under the covers and stare at the ceilin for a few minutes. Then before I know it, I'm passed out and sleepin again, but only for a little while, and when I wake up again, the gray light a dawn peaks thru the little openings that frame the window shade. James is awake. With his hands behind his head, he's starin at the ceilin like I was a little while ago. Swede's still asleep but he'll be comin around any minute now. James gets outa bed and goes over and raises the shade and looks out at the gray mornin. We spend the next hour gettin our bedrolls together and takin turns washin up in the little sink in the corner. The toilet's down the hall, and we take turns usin that, too.

By seven-thirty we're back on the street. The flophouse is close to another train yard, not the one we came into. Since its so close, we take a walk over there to check out the traffic. We talk to a hobo that's headin for Missouri, and he says this line is the Atchison, Topeka and the Santa Fe which goes north outa Texas. He tells us we want the Southern Pacific that goes outa the other yard, the one we came into last night. Then he tells us we better get over there in a hurry cuz theres a freight headin for Phoenix at around eight oclock. So, we get outa there, not knowin what time it is exactly, but knowin we're cuttin it close and we better get a move on.

We're half runnin to get there when we pass a fillin station with a clock above the door to the office; it says five after eight. We slow down a little, but we're still walkin pretty fast when we enter the yard five minutes later. Things are lookin real quiet. A couple hobos are hangin around a couple tracks over. We hike over to em. They tell us theyre headin east, and one of em says he thinks it was the Phoenix freight train that just pulled out a few minutes ago. He says there were quite a few riders.

"Damn," James says. "We missed it."

"I been around a few days," says the hobo, "and it looks to me like theres usually two freights a day goin west, one at eight in the mornin and the other at five in the afternoon. You could get that one this afternoon, but then you'd be travelin at night, and we all know how cold its been gettin. Last night's frost aint hardly melted yet. Hell, tomorrow's the first day a winter."

"Say, are you sure about that schedule?" James says to the hobo. "Therell be another one outa here at eight tomorrow morning?"

"Theres been one every day at eight for the last five days I been watchin. Weekends they started from right here. Week days they been comin thru from the east."

"Well, I'll be damned," James says. "We can try again tomorrow, boys." Then to the hobo, "Thanks a lot, pal."

We start walkin outa the yard, headin back into town. We find a streetcar stop bench and sit down and make our plans, and what we decide to do is spend the rest a the day and night across the border. We heard about a town over there called Ciudad Juarez. We figure our money'll go further over there like when we stayed in Acuña. But we gotta make sure we get back to that yard by seven-thirty in the mornin come hell or high water. With that worked out, we start off goin toward the river. Theres a wind comin up. We pass the fillin station we passed before, and James pops inside the little glassed-in office and gets directions to the border from the attendant who is tryin to stay outa the wind.

"All we've gotta do is go down here a couple blocks until we get to the Good Neighbor Bridge, and that takes us across the Rio Grande and over into Juarez," James tells us.

211

Jerome Arthur

Since we found out we aint goin west today, Swede's taken on the most discouraged look I ever seen. I'm ready to get to California, too, but who knows, maybe our stayin here another day is good. It aint gonna kill us, that's for sure. The way the wind is pickin up, we're probly better off not bein on a boxcar anyway. The conditions aint the best for ridin the rails today. James says that train we missed is gonna get scoured by the wind and sand when it goes thru New Mexico and Arizona. In that case I'm glad we're not on it. Its bad enough tryin to walk in this damn wind right here in town. Its dry and cold, and every so often it hurls some small piece a litter—a candy wrapper—past us. No doubt it'd blow right thru the open spaces on any boxcar.

We're on South Stanton Street, comin up on a bridge. A streetcar glides past. Sparks flash off its trolley and get caught just for a second by the gustin wind, dyin out before they can be carried off. As we start goin up on the bridge, the wind blows like crazy, so that when we're right above the river, we have to turn our heads away from it and protect our eyes with our forearms bent over our eyebrows cuz its blowin sand from the river bank right in our faces. We move thru it until we come down on the other side into an enclosed area where a Mexi-can's sittin opposite a turnstile next to one a those glass boxes you see in streetcars and buses where you put yer fare. Next to the box is a sign that says "1¢"; damned if they dont charge you to cross the border. I get the money out and theres five pennies in with the change. I give Swede and James each one, and I take one myself. I put the last two back in my

212

inside pocket. We drop em in the glass box, and one at a time we walk thru the turnstile. We're back in Mexico again.

The wind is blowin just as hard in Juárez as it was in El Paso. I notice over here they put that little accent mark over the "á" in the name a the town. You can see how this whole layout is right outa the old west. When I look at the mountains, I half expect to see the silhouette of a mounted cowboy up on the ridge, the guy that came before us. They was the first white men to roam around the west; we're followin in their footsteps. They was saddle tramps; we're rail bums. The same and different all at the same time.

As we look around for someplace to go to get outa the wind, I'm noticin that Juárez is packed a little tighter than El Paso. Theres houses on almost every square inch a ground in the tiny city blocks. No yards anywhere. Off to our right we see some kinda stadium. James says its a bull ring. A little further on we come to a bus depot. Theres little kids everywhere sellin everything from gum to shoe shines. One kid even offered his "virgin sister" for "a good price." We get past em and take a right on that corner and we're on Avenida diez y seis de Septiembre. In the next block I see a sign that says, "Hotel."

The sign painted in the window says single rooms are fifty centavos. I dont know how much that is in American money. We walk in the front door and are greeted by a smilin desk clerk. Havin the same trouble with his limited Spanish as he had with Virgilio in Acuña, James manages to get us two rooms separated by a bathroom, and its only costin us thirty cents.

213

When we get into our rooms, I see this is a much better deal than what we had last night. Right now, its just nice to have a place where we can stay outa the wind, and even from inside our rooms, we can still hear it howlin and poundin. We spend most a the afternoon right here, and around sundown the wind lightens up some. Its still breezy out there, but it aint nearly as strong and gusty as it was when we checked into this joint.

"You fellas feel like gettin out?" James says. "It looks like now's our chance to go out and look around Juárez."

Me and Swede are both past ready to get out. We been cooped up in here all afternoon. The three of us start movin around gettin ready to go. Its still plenty cold even tho the wind has died down quite a bit. We put our hands in our pockets and head back in the same the direction we came from. When we get back into the center a downtown, we see this real old church next to a park and plaza. Theres a plaque over near the mission building, and I walk over there and read it. It says the mission was built in 1659. Wow! Now that's old. We keep goin back the way we came, and we turn down another busy street. A lot's happenin here. Since they aint got prohibition down here, theres plenty a joints sellin whiskey, wine and beer right out in the open. That dont mean we can go in em, tho. Just cuz the stuff's legal down here dont mean theyre gonna let kids hang around where they sell it. And the booze aint the only reason they dont want kids in there. As we're passin the open door a one a the saloons, I get a good look inside and see a naked girl on a stage with a bar

214

circling all around it. She aint completely naked. She's got on a pair a high heel shoes and a pair a underpants pulled down around her thighs just above her knees. We stand there for a while catchin glimpses thru the swingin doors when someone goes in or comes out. Most a the people comin and goin look like American soldiers. There must be an army base around here some-where. Seems like there was a lota soldiers back over in El Paso, too.

We walk a little further down the street, lookin in the shop windows as we go. Its mostly cheap jewelry: rings, cuff links, and earrings; and leather: wallets, belts, and purses. We go to the end a the street and double back, movin toward our hotel. One a the shops we pass is a diner. We go in and sit down at the counter and order some tacos. When we pay the bill for that dinner, we're down to thirteen dollars and some change. We're gonna have to get to the coast pretty quick.

Back in our rooms, we clean up and get comfortable and sit down to do some readin. Its still fairly early when I doze off for the night. That wind just took it outa me, and besides if we're gonna get up early in the mornin, we better get to bed early.

Twenty-four

As we pull outa El Paso at eight oclock in the mornin, I realize how glad I am that we're leavin. I liked Del Rio better. For one thing the weather was a lot warmer there than here. Also, it was smaller and more down home. I have to say that El Paso does look pretty from this distance up on the mountain. Last night wasnt as cold as the night before. Clouds block the sun today, and it dont seem to be warmin up a-tall. It must be gettin close to ten oclock, and its just a little warmer than it was at daybreak.

We're goin north and I think we might be in New Mexico by now. Off to our left is a mountain range. Huge rocks and boulders everywhere. This is desolate country. As I'm watchin it roll by thru a crack in the boards of the door, I hear the mournful song of James's harmonica thru the rumble a the boxcar and the whoosh of air skimmin past us on the outside. I lean back against a bale a hay and bundle up in my wool army blanket. I'm feelin real alone now. If we was to get run off by bulls here, we'd be in a heap a shit. We could be stranded for a long time or even die out here, and nobody'd ever know we was gone, swallowed by the desert. I cant think such things. I gotta believe I'm not gonna die alone in some rocky red desert in New Mexico. I just got to come to a better end than that.

We steam thru one small town, and about a half hour later, as Swede just happens to be lookin out the crack of open door, we cross the continental divide. He saw the sign about a quarter mile before we got to it, and he called us over to look at it. It says, "Continental Divide, Elevation 4,585."

"Is that the highest spot in the forty-eight states?" Swede says to James.

"No. That's actually the spot on the North American continent where the water on the east side runs off to the Atlantic Ocean, and the water on the west side goes to the Pacific Ocean. Some experts figured it all out. In places where the rails run alongside a river, like up in Colorado, you can actually see the river change directions at the Continental Divide."

"That's swell," I say, and it *is* somethin to get excited about. "That means we're in the west now, and California cant be too far away."

"You could say that," James says. "I'll bet we're not too far from Arizona right now, and you know what comes after that."

Its colder'n shit, so we close the door and crawl back into our corner and huddle up in our blankets. The next time I look out, we're rollin thru a little town called Benson, and I think we're in Arizona. Even tho we still have to keep wrapped up in our blankets to stay warm, it seems a little warmer than it was just a little while ago. I'm guessin its around two, three oclock.

217

Jerome Arthur

We roll along the rails for another hour, and we're in Tucson where the train stops. We scramble off the boxcar while its still movin. James takes the lead and we follow im across a couple sets a tracks and up an embankment, and we're on a city street. Since we stopped movin, I can feel how much warmer it is here than it was back where we just come from. This is more like it was in Del Rio. Its got so warm that the three of us are unbuttonin our coats. This aint a big town, bigger'n Del Rio, but smaller'n El Paso from the look of it. The yard's right in the center a town, so here we are. We just kinda walk around a bit, look the place over, dont see much, a sure bet we dont see anything we can make a buck off of. Its real pretty tho, desert warm and colored light tan with tinges of the red we saw in New Mexico. The sun's gettin close to the western horizon, and I bet the sunset and the sunrise on this desert are really somethin to see. We're gonna find out.

After hangin around town for a while, we head back to the yard to see if maybe we can find a hobo jungle we can spend the night in. Since its so warm, it might not be too bad stayin outside. Course I dont know how cold its gonna be at four in the mornin. We damn sure cant afford no more rooms. We got the money, but we aint got it to spare. We should hang onto what little we got left. It might come in handy when we get to Los Angeles, and that could even be tomorrow. We're that close. As we're walkin along back toward the yard, we pass a grocery store. We go in and pick up three cans a Camp-bells chicken noodle soup, a small loaf a bread and a quart bottle a milk. All

218

of it cost thirty-three cents, leavin us thirteen dollars and twenty-ninety cents. Actually, we did okay since New Orleans. Sure, we spent a lota dough, but we sure stayed in some nice spots, like the cabin in Acuña. And we been eatin' good, too.

We go back to the yard. Over on the other side near a bridge, we see smoke risin into the early evenin sky from behind some tall bushes. We walk over there and sure enough, theres three campfires. One of em has only one-person sittin next to it, so we move over that way, but we dont even have to ask im if we can join im. He sees us comin, and as we approach, he says,

"Ah, gentlemen, welcome to my humble abode." He dont stand up, but he takes off his slightly tattered, silk top hat, nods his head, and with a sweepin gesture of his right arm, top hat in hand, offers us places next to his campfire. "Spangler Dillon at your service," he says.

"My name's James. These are my friends: Antoine and Swede. We just picked some things up at a grocery store. How would you like to have some dinner with us?"

We shake hands around, and I like his handshake. He has a good solid grip, no dead fish.

"Why, I'd be delighted to partake in a repast with you boys," he says. He's wearin a heavy, black wool coat that, when he's standin up, hangs to about two inches above the knees of his charcoal gray wool trousers. He picks up a backpack by the log he's restin against and pulls out a saucepan and a can opener. He's heavy, like he's too well-fed for such hard times. "I suppose one can never be too prepared for such unex-

219

pected gratuities. You'll forgive my effusiveness, but its been some time since I've enjoyed such a lavish feast. Well, shall we prepare dinner, gentlemen?"

He takes the two cans a soup from James and bites into em with his can opener. Me and Swede go scroungin around for more wood for the fire. James takes the empty soup cans and walks off toward the switchman's shack where theres a water faucet. Me and Swede get the fire goin better, and Dillon sets the sauce pan down on a jury-rigged grate he's got set up over the fire. James comes back and dumps the two cans a water into the sauce pan while Dillon stirs. When the soup simmers, Dillon gets a metal bowl outa his pack, and we pour some into it and into the three empty cans.

Dillon takes a jug a booze outa his pack and offers us all a shot. James has one, but me and Swede dont want one. We're drinkin the milk we bought earlier, tryin to get rid of it before it goes sour. James is drinkin some, too, but not Dillon. He's only drinkin his whiskey. When we get done eatin, James sits back and plays his mouth organ, and Dillon reaches into his pack and brings out a deck a cards.

"Have you gentlemen ever been witness to any magic or slate of hand techniques?" he says.

I look at Swede, and if I'm as bug-eyed as he is, the two of us must be a funny sight. Hell, I dont even know what slate of hand is, but I dont wanna say so cuz I dont wanna look dumb. So, I just shrug my shoulders, and so does Swede.

"Well, let me demonstrate," he says. And for the next hour, with the mournful backdrop of the music

220

trailin outa James's harmonica, Dillon performs some unbelievable card tricks. I cant figure how he does it, but you can pick any card, and put it back in the deck and he'll find it every time. He also does some magic tricks with a cane and scarves and his top hat.

"Boy, you sure are a magician, aint yuh?" I say. He looks as good to me as the magician I seen last year at the Pantages Theater in downtown Minneapolis. "You should take it on stage. Yuh know, get into show business."

"Ah, lad, so much easier said than done. Just last week I terminated a two-year sojourn in Hollywood. In two years, I couldnt sell my act to anyone. I had to depart, and now I do not know where I shall end. Perhaps New York. I think there might still be some work for me on Broadway or more remotely, Vaudeville. Now that's a dying art."

"Well, that's too bad," I say. "Will you keep on doin' magic tricks?"

"Oh, yes indeed," he says. "I think I'll always find an audience, as I did so many times on the corner of Hollywood and Vine, but indubitably there would be more satisfaction in receiving some sort of monetary remuneration for my performance, somethin more than the mere pennies dropped on the sidewalk at my feet by curious pedestrians."

"What kinda place is Los Angeles?" I say. "I mean, did you like Hollywood, the weather and all?"

"Oh, yes indeed. I daresay its the land of milk and honey. Its sunny and warm most of the time; the boulevards are wide and lined with palm trees sixty feet tall. And the blue Pacific is so docile, a marvelous

221

playground with its wide beaches. I think you gentlemen will enjoy it immensely."

"And what about jobs?" I ask. "I mean not
magician jobs, but regular jobs."

"Are you not aware of the fact that theres a
depression in progress? Jobs are quite scarce in all lo-
cations and professions. College professors are selling
pencils on street corners. However, I have a plan for
you to get some compensation, if limited."

"How's that?" I say.

I'm startin to get the hang of his speech and
vocabulary. An hour ago, I wouldnt've understood that
he was goin to give me a line on how to make some
dough when we get to Los Angeles.

"Well, whenever I would find myself in need
of funds, what I would do was go to various studios
and get day work as an extra. They pay two dollars a
day, which isnt extravagant, but for me its more than
adequate, and the extra added attraction was that it was
work that was closely related to my chosen profes-
sion."

By now James quit playin and is kinda listenin
in on our conversation. You could see im perk up when
Dillon started talkin about studios and extras and the
like. Finally, he says,

"You know an actress named Lorraine Morrison? She's been in a couple of B-movies."

"Hmm. Morrison, you say? I dont recognize
the name, but I daresay there is a plethora of young
actresses in Hollywood, so one can hardly know them
all. Why do you inquire?"

222

"Oh, she's just a lady I knew once, and I'd kind of like to look her up when I get to the coast."

"Well, if she's there, I have every confidence you'll locate her. As I said, there are many people working in the business, but theyre all located in one place. And who might you lads be looking for in Hollywood?"

"Nobody," Swede says. "We aint goin to Hollywood; we're goin to Seal Beach. My aunt lives there. Gonna stay with her for a while, get jobs, and then maybe find a place of our own."

"Where, pray tell, is Seal Beach?" Dillon asks.

"Near a town called Long Beach. I seen it on a map once."

"Oh, way out in the country."

"I dont know," Swede says. "I never been there myself, but I heard from letters she wrote my ma that she lives right on the beach."

"Ah, the beach in Southern California. Easy living among the palms. I never visited Long Beach or any of the other beaches in that general area, so I really cant give a first hand report of what it might be like, but if its anything like Santa Monica, you wont be disappointed. I've been there."

"Oh boy. I cant wait to get there," Swede says.

"Well, it wont be long now," James says. "If we get lucky tomorrow morning, we could be pulling into a yard somewhere in Los Angeles by tomorrow night, which means you could get some sand in your shoes by day after tomorrow."

I'm just layin back takin it all in and gettin excited thinkin about it, how far we've come and the short distance left to go. The night is comin on, and all four of us get our little spots staked out around the fire, spreadin out our bedrolls and smoothin out the ground we're gonna sleep on. We make one more sweep around us and get enough wood to keep the fire goin for a little while longer. Then we bundle up in our blankets and go to sleep. I wake up one time durin the night to discover that its cold but not freezin. Its really kinda comfortable as long as I keep my blanket wrapped around me.

Twenty-five

We got lucky. We said goodbye to Dillon and hopped a freight at around nine oclock. This mornin I seen one a the most beautiful sunrises ever. It was prettier'n anything I couldve expected or hoped for, all red and gold bands rustin together along the whole eastern horizon. And with the sun comes warmer weather. The way things are heatin up right now, it could turn out to be a hot day, but then we got a lota miles to travel, so I guess we could run into just about anything, even rain. It *is* winter, and with these high temperatures, I tend to forget that. I know it aint nothin like this back home right now.

We're only on the road for a couple hours, and then the train stops in Phoenix. We get off and wander around the yard for about a half hour lookin for somethin else outa there, but we cant find anything. Theyre loadin some big wooden crates onto the train we just got off of, and they aint separated the engine and tender from the boxcars neither, so maybe theyll be pullin out pretty soon goin west, maybe all the way west. When they finish loadin one a the cars and start on the next, I sneak over and have a look at the crates on the loaded car. Theres an invoice stapled to each one. I climb up into the car to get a good look at it. It says all kinds a things on it, like what it is and how many, but I only notice one thing, and thats the destination. It says Los Angeles.

Jerome Arthur

I scramble down off the train and go back over to James and Swede and tell em the good news. So now we just gotta sit around and wait for the train to start rollin and away we'll go. From the looks of it, its gonna take em some time to get loaded, so rather than just sit there, we go a couple blocks outa the yard where we find a diner that's in an old trolley car. We spend about fifty cents and get us some turkey sandwiches and some pop to take with us back to the train yard.

It takes em about another hour to get all the cargo loaded, and the train starts rollin as soon as they slide the door shut on the last loaded car, which is the one we want cuz it aint full like the other ones. So, we trot alongside until James gets a leg up enough to get the door back open, and me and Swede jump right in behind our bedrolls. Once we get settled in, we start lookin over the freight. Its warm enough that we dont have to stay bundled up in the corner. The invoice on one a the boxes says its blankets from the Salt River Indian Reservation.

When we was doin' all that work for Miss Dupree in New Orleans, we noticed she had two claw hammers in her tools. Somehow James knew we'd be needin one a those hammers, so he asked her if he could take one and she said yes. So ol' James takes that claw hammer outa his bedroll and breaks open one a the crates. When we get it opened, sure enough, its brand-new Indian blankets with different patterns and designs on em. We each grab one, and then James closes up the box, but we cant seal it proper, so we slide it back behind another one so you cant see right

226

away that its been opened. I sure hope the Indians already got their money, cuz I'd feel real bad if we was taken from them and not the guy that's gonna profit from sellin the blankets. We unroll our bedrolls and then roll em back up with our new blankets inside. Its so warm and dry that we dont need any heavy blankets or jackets right now. We coulda used these new blankets back in El Paso or when we was goin thru Chicago.

So, we prop ourselves up against the cartons and watch the desert slide by. Theres still plenty a mountains all around us, and big rocks and boulders, too. This is the real wild west. I half expect Geron-imo or Cochise to come ridin down off one a these mountains or outa one a these canyons leadin a tribe a warriors. Me and Swede are wide eyed. James is wawaing on his harmonica.

By the time we get to Yuma, the afternoon is movin along. I hope we'll be able to ride this freight all the way to Los Angeles. Theres only two things that can stop us now; we could get rousted or the train could stop and lay over someplace. If we have to travel at night, it shouldnt be too cold, and even if it is, we got all these blankets to keep us warm. We're on a roll now, and we wanna keep it goin. All three of us would be happy as hell if we could make it into Los Angeles tonight.

We cross a river as we leave Yuma, and then it seems we're kinda goin north. I think we're in California now. The sun is goin down off to our left. This is the most desolate desert we've seen so far. Lookin out the door on the left, I see these big sand dunes. It looks

227

like some a those scenes from one a Rudolph Valentino's movies. I cant help thinkin I'll see an oasis with palm trees and date trees and a cool-water spring. The last couple nights the moon's been about three quarters full. I expect its gonna be the same tonight, so it should be easy to see stuff in the desert night. We dont exactly come onto an oasis, but a little further up the line we watch the sun sink into a pretty good size lake. Leavin the lake behind, we continue to roll north. As it gets dark, we see the lights of a small town up ahead. The temperature goes down with the sun, so we unwrap our bedrolls and bundle up in our old and new blankets.

The lights are the town a Indio. We dont stop there, but as we're rollin thru the station, I read the sign above the platform. The train picks up speed again when we get clear a the station. We bent a little to the left, so I guess we're headin west again. The moon's behind us and the north star is on our right. Feels like we're gettin there. We're still travelin thru desert and is it ever beautiful! I cant decide which was prettier, the sunrise or the sunset. Some a the colors I seen were really too much to even try to describe. And the desert at night, so cool and alive. It seemed real dead durin the day. The desert animals must go into hidin under the white glare of the daytime sun, cuz we didnt see anything then. Now we're seein jack rabbits scurryin around by the light a the moon, and every once in a while I hear somethin howlin. James says its a coyote.

On the left is another small town twinklin in the dark desert night. We dont go thru it, but we can see it off in the distance. Not twenty minutes go by and we're comin to another town. We go right thru it, only slowin down a bit. We seem to be climbin, but not for long. When we crest the hill, we're lookin down on a pretty good size town. The lights seem to be spread out quite a bit, and beyond em its dark again. The train rolls down outa the mountains, zigzaggin toward the lights. When we reach em, we slide right past em. Now its a succession of one small town after another. Only one of em has a station, and as we pass it, I read "Po-mona" on the sign hangin above the platform. As we pick up speed goin outa the station, the train bends to the left and into a desolate flatland area. We're bendin back to the right around these gentle rollin hills. Next we go thru a heavy industrial area. Well, I guess that says it. We must be on the outskirts a Los Angeles now. I wonder how far it is to the end a the line.

"Well, boys, we're on our way now," James says. "We'll probably be in downtown Los Angeles in another hour or so."

With that news me and Swede let out a cheer. Now it seems like we're passin thru a town every ten minutes. We'll be rollin along in darkness for a while, and then the twinklin lights of another town appear up ahead. We cross over a couple dry creek beds. After about the fifth town, the intervals of darkness become shorter, and the lights start to run together. We must be in the actual city a Los Angeles. Its all lights and hous-es and city streets. Then we pass thru the residential neighborhoods and come into another industrial area and then a huge train yard. Up ahead we see what must be downtown Los Angeles. Theres one tall building that looks as tall as the Foshay Tower. High up on it theres a triangle of Christmas lights that looks like a

229

lighted Christmas tree. We cross over a great big channel (maybe a couple hundred feet wide) with just a
trickle a water runnin down the center. Now the train
starts slowin down as it bends to the right and coasts
into a train yard that's almost as big as the one in Chicago. We jump off as the train comes to a stop.

We go up ahead to a bridge where theres a few
campfires burnin. Theres quite a few hobos still awake
and talkin over smokes and coffee. We find us a place
by ourselves and spread our bedrolls out, and cuz we're
so tired from bein on the rails all day, we drop off on
the spot. I dont know what time it is, but I'd guess nine
or ten oclock. Gettin these new blankets was a swell
deal. Now we can use our old ones to lay on top of and
then cover up with the new ones. It aint a mattress, but
it beats layin on the cold hard ground like we been
doin'. As tired as I am, I cant seem to fall asleep. I'm
so excited to be here. I keep thinkin about all the things
we gotta do, like go to Hollywood and look up Lorraine. We gotta find out where Seal Beach is and how
to get there, and then we gotta go there. Then we gotta
find us a way to make some dough. And before we do
any a that, I gotta send a wire to Ma, let her know I'm
okay.

All a this is racin thru my mind as I lay there
awake under the stars. Its chilly, but not so much that
we're freezin our asses off.

Twenty-six

Once I do fall asleep, its a deep sleep with no dreams. I wake up to the sound a some tramps movin around in the grainy light of early dawn. Theyre scroungin around for some wood to throw onto their fire. I look at James and Swede, and theyre openin their eyes, too. These guys rummagin around sure are makin a lota noise.

"Hey," one of em yells past us to the other. "Over here theres some tree branches on the ground."

The other one runs past us, almost trippin over Swede, under the bridge to the other side. The train yard and the river bed we went over last night on our way in are on this side a the street; the other side slopes up a wooded hill. It looks like some kinda forest right here in the middle a town. Those two hobos are up there scurryin around lookin for scraps a wood for their fire.

We get out from under our blankets and stretch the stiffness outa our joints. Its gettin lighter. The sun should be comin up any minute. It *is* gonna come up; the sky is crystal clear, not a cloud anywhere. A passenger train goes clickety-clackin thru the yard, blank stares lookin out empty windows. James stops one a the hobos comin down outa the woods with an arm load a branches.

"You know how to get to Hollywood?" he asks.

"Sure nuff. I been there a couple times since I been in this town," the hobo says. "Yuh just go down North Broadway here. That's this here street. Go down about a mile until you get to Sunset. Take a right on Sunset and go about five more miles and yer there. Its a long way to go on foot, but its mostly flat. Yuh aint got no hills to climb, ceptin maybe some little ones. Yuh got any dough, yuh can take the streetcar."

"Thanks," James tells im. "You boys ready for Hollywood? Wha'da yuh say?"

"Sounds easy enough to get there," I say. "We migh's well get goin on it. Yer as anxious to see yer wife as me and Swede are to get to his aunt's place, and the sooner we do the first, its that much quicker that we'll get to the second."

"Right," he says. "Lets go."

So here we are three and a half weeks from when we pulled outa Minneapolis, over two thousand miles away and now we're headin to Hollywood. The sun comes up, castin a bright light onto the tall building we saw last night. In the sunlight its white as elephant tusks, very different from the Foshay tower which is dark and sooty from the coal burnin winters. Hell, around here, it dont even look like they need indoor heat.

We roll up our bedrolls and climb up the embankment to the street. Right next to the railin as you start to cross the bridge, theres a sign screwed to the bridge abutment that says, "Los Angeles River." On the other side a the bridge, we can see where the street forks left and right. We walk that way to the middle a the span, and when we get right over the river, we stop

232

and look down and see only a trickle of water runnin down the center a what's maybe a couple hundred-foot-wide weed-choked channel. Compared to the Mississippi back home, its a sorry excuse for a river.

Over to the right and a level up from the river, the hobos are stokin their fires. From this spot on the middle a the bridge, we have the most beautiful view of the snow-capped mountains surroundin this valley, and in between theres rollin hills here and there, some with houses built on em, some only wooded and green just like this one across the street from the rail yard.

When we get to the other side a the bridge, we check out the street sign. The street goin to the left is Pasadena Avenue, the one goin to the right is North Broadway. A half block down North Broadway theres a sign that says, "Lincoln Heights District" with the official city seal in the center of it. We turn around and cross back over the bridge, headin in the direction of the tall building.

When we get back across the bridge, I see that North Broadway is one carved out terrace in the side of a small mountain. The train yard's the next terrace down before you come to the river bed. As we move down the street, I notice some houses built right up against the mountain on our right across the street. I wonder what that mountain is anyway right in the middle a town like that. It finally starts levelin out when we pass a Catholic school and church. The tracks are still hard on our left but down below us a good thirty feet or so. All the tracks in the yard come together until its just one track, and that one banks off to the left and disappears as we come into Chinatown. Now its all a flat, congested downtown. A yellow streetcar glides past. If I was by myself, I could hop right on the rear and the conductor would never see me. Its hard for three guys to do that, especially when one of em is as big as Swede.

A couple blocks past Chinatown and we come to Sunset Boulevard, just like the hobo said.

"I'd sure like to go to the top a that," I say, pointin at the tall building. Its only a couple blocks away now. We're standin on the corner a Broadway and Sunset.

"Well, we'll just have to try and do it at some point," James says. "Its a bit early right now. Probably not open yet."

We start walkin up Sunset. Theres a newsstand about a half block up. The man sellin the papers is inside this wooden box of a shack with newspapers and magazines everywhere you look: over his head, on the counter in front of im, stacked up on the ground in front a the shack, in racks hangin on the side a the shack. One a the newspapers that's stacked on the sidewalk has a weather map and a listin of the temperatures around the country in the lower right-hand corner a the front page. All I gotta do is lean down and look at it without even pickin it up to see that the weather back home is pretty cold. In Minneapolis it only got up to thirty-nine degrees yesterday. The low was nineteen, and it snowed. Its probly only about sixty-five degrees here right now, but that's a hell of a lot better'n thirty-nine.

We keep walking up Sunset. A couple blocks up we go in a coffee and doughnut shop. We sit down

at the counter and order three coffees and three doughnuts. This is our breakfast. As we're sittin at the counter, I'm starin at the traffic goin by out on the street,
and I see a streetcar pass by with a sign in the little side
window next to the front door that says, "Hollywood."

We finish our coffee and go back out on the
sidewalk. The coffee shop is on the corner a Sunset and
Bunker Hill Avenue and lookin down that street we see
the gold and black tower of another tall building. We
go one block up to Temple Street and from there downtown Los Angeles is spread out in front of us. The tall
white building is just two blocks to our left. We got a
good view of the other tall building straight ahead. Its a
lot different from the other white one. For one thing it
aint as tall as the white one, and it looks like its made
outa black granite trimmed on the corners in some kinda gold plate. The tower on top a the building has a
vertical sign that looks like it says "Richfield." Its kinda hard to read at this distance. We head back to Sunset
and walk for maybe another mile or so, and in that time
another streetcar passes.

"This is turnin into a pretty long walk," I say.
"Lets get on the next streetcar that comes along. What
can it cost, a couple pennies maybe?"

"That's a real swell idea," Swede says. "I'm
tired a walkin."

So, we keep walkin, and sure enough, not fifteen minutes goes by and here comes another streetcar
goin to Hollywood. We're just past the middle a the
block, so we gotta run to get to the safety zone at the
next corner in time to meet the streetcar. I get a quarter
out, and when we climb aboard, I ask the conductor

235

how much it is, and he tells me two cents. So, I ask im for change for the quarter, and from a changer on his belt, he clicks out ten pennies, a dime and a nickel. I give James and Swede each two cents, and when we drop em into the glass box, the motorman asks us if we want transfers, so we take transfers. We sit down on the hard-wooden seats that are actually pretty comfortable cuz a the way theyre curved to the shape of yer body when yer sittin down. As we glide along, I gaze out the window at the passin scene. What a beautiful place this is! All these stucco houses (houses, huh! mansions more like) are so white and clean lookin. Their red tile roofs make em look so happy. Christmas trees decorate the picture windows of each one. And the palm trees along the boulevards are a site to see.

The streetcar takes a sharp left, and a block later theres a sign on the side a the road exactly like the one we saw back on Broadway in Lincoln Heights that says, "Hollywood District." So, this is it, home of the stars and their movin pictures. We go a few more blocks and the conductor calls out, "Western Avenue." Shortly after this stop, I'm lookin out the window, and who should I see but Max Nyquist, a kid me and Swede knew in school. He also lived in the neighborhood, only two blocks away.

"Hey, Swede," I say. "Take a look at that, would yuh?"

We both know Max, and I guess he's an okay kid, but he's just different from us. For one thing, he's a real student when it comes to school. Smart as hell. Reads everything. So, we dont hang around with im, but we've always been friendly with im.

236

"Its Max," he says. "Wonder what the hell he's doin' here. We should stop and talk to im. He might have some news from home."

I pull the buzzer cord, and we get off at the next stop. Max is headin right toward us, and I see from the way he looks compared to us, this is gonna be embarrassin. He's all clean and dressed nice, while me and Swede look like a couple ragamuffins, and James looks like some kinda down-and-out bum. We get within ten feet of im and he still dont recognize us until I say,

"Hey, Max, how yuh doin'?"

He acts like he cant believe its us way out here two thousand miles away from home.

"What are you fellas doin' here?" he says still actin like he dont believe we could really be here.

"We ran away last month, but what're you doin' here?" I say.

"I wondered why I never saw you around school or in the neighborhood after Thanksgiving. So, you ran away from home, huh? I came out with my father. He's got a chance to work in pictures. His brother works for one of the big studios, and he told my father about a possible job opening, so he and I came out on the train last week. We just arrived in town yesterday. We left Mother and Erik at home. If it works out and he gets the job, then we'll send for them. If he doesnt get the job, we'll head back home. So how did you fellas get here?"

"Took the train, too, freight trains," Swede says, a bit on the sarcastic side. "We been on the road three and a half weeks and only got into town last night."

"You hear anything about my stepdad?" I ask im. "Is he hurt bad?"

"What are you talking about? Why would he be hurt? I see him walking around the neighborhood all the time. He doesnt look hurt to me."

"Wouldnt you just know it," I say, more to myself than to anybody else. Then to Max, "The son of a bitch's head's harder'n a goddamn Louisville Slugger. Last time I seen im, he was layin in a pool a blood on the dinin room floor cuz I put im there with my baseball bat. How about my ma? She okay, yuh think?"

"You know, now that you mention it, I dont know," he says. "I really havent seen her at all. In fact, I havent seen her doughnuts anywhere around lately. I really hadn't thought anything of it until you just now called it to my attention."

Swede starts askin im about his own family, and I drift off to one side wonderin about Ma, and what I'm supposed to do now. I guess I should sit down and write her a letter to at least let her know I'm okay. If she's feelin bad cuz she dont know how I am, then a little note would sure make her feel better. That's the first thing I'll do when I get to Swede's aunt's house. After givin Swede the lowdown on his family, Max tells us that he's on his way to a filmin of an "Our Gang" episode at a studio down near Vine Street.

"My uncle came by our hotel to pick up my father to take him to a meeting with some other people about the job. My father gave me a quarter and my uncle gave me a pass to go watch this filming, so I

238

thought I'd just go look it over. Why dont you fellas come on along. I bet I could get you in with this pass."

"I dont know," I say, glancin at James. "We got some stuff to do."

But James is already wavin me off.

"No, no. You boys go ahead and go to the show. I'll scout around on my own for a while, and then I'll meet you afterward."

So, all four of us walk the seven blocks or so to Vine. When James leaves us, he says he'll meet us right here in three hours. Max shows his pass at the studio gate, and the guard waves all three of us in, so we walk into this big lot with warehouse kinda buildings here and there. These aint warehouses like the ones we worked at along the riverfront in New Orleans. These warehouses aint just tin buildings, but regular buildings, mostly stucco. Movin toward the back a the lot behind the last two buildings, we come upon a crowd a people with cameras and other equipment. Theyre all standin around on "Elm Street U.S.A." with white picket fences, green lawns, shade trees and nice houses. But the houses only have one wall propped up by two-by-fours.

We move in a little closer to the people, and in among the crowd, there they are, the Little Rascals in the flesh. We're just kinda hangin around, unnoticed by anybody when all of a sudden a loud voice calls out,

"Ready on the set!"

Then everybody backs away leavin Stymie, Chubby, and Wheezer on the sidewalk. Theyre all set up in a pose. Then a man steps up with a split piece a slate with some writin on it that says, "Dogs is Dogs,"

239

and holdin it up, he scissors the top part up and clacks it down, sayin, "action" at the same time. Then the three kids start actin a scene from the movie theyre makin. Farina and Mary Ann are behind the director watchin the scene with the rest of us. The cameras are goin, and they make it all the way thru the scene without stoppin, and when its over, all the people split off in different directions while a few are millin around the area. A couple a the men are talkin about how theyre gonna set up the next scene. We're just kinda hangin around when one a the men looks our way and walks over to us. Lookin straight at me as he gets closer, he says,

"How'd you like to be an extra in this picture we're shootin' here? We'll pay you two dollars. Your dressed perfectly for the part. We wont even have to make you up."

He's only talkin to me, not includin Swede or Max in the conversation. I guess he only wants me and not them.

"Well, I guess so," I say. "I could sure use the loot."

"You'll be perfect. You've got the right lingo, too. Follow me," he says as he starts walkin me off toward one a the buildings.

"Tell James what happened, and I'll see yuh when they let me go," I tell Swede as I walk off with the man.

We go into the building and down a hall to a room where theres four other boys. One of em is sittin in a chair in front of a mirror, and some queer-lookin guy is puttin makeup on his face so he looks dirty and

240

usin a comb to muss his hair. All four of em are all tattered and dirty just like me, except mine's the real thing. Theirs is just costumes and makeup.

"Here's another one," the man with me says to the queer. "That's all five of em. See if you cant have em ready in half an hour."

He leaves. I ask the kid closest to me how he came to be here, and he tells me he just happened to be passin by on the street when the man that put the arm on me put the arm on him, too. As soon as the queer quits foolin around with our clothes and our faces, the five of us march across the lot to a cafe-teria where everybody's havin lunch. We all get trays and go thru the line fillin em with some real swell food.

241

Twenty-seven

Us boys are the last ones to finish lunch, and when we do, a girl looks to be in her early twenties meets us at the cafeteria door and walks us back to the set where the crowd a actors and crew are gatherin to do the next scene. The other four boys are a couple years younger'n me. I think they picked me and not Swede or Max cuz I'm so little. I'm closer to the same size as these other fellas. After the queer finished fixin me up, I look younger than I really am.

We're standin on the edge a the crowd watchin a fella direct a scene without cameras runnin. They go thru it three times, and then they do it with the cameras rollin. I see Swede and Max over on the other side a the set. A couple more spectators joined em. After about an hour, our guide, the young girl (a real knock-out, too, with her long dark hair flowin down onto her breast when she straightens up from leanin forward) takes us back to the room where they did the make-up on us, and then we just hang around there for the next hour or so. Its where I left my bedroll, which is where my book is, so after about fifteen minutes of just sittin (I aint got nothin to talk about with these other little kids they got me hangin around with), I pull the book outa the bedroll, and start readin. I dont know how long we been hangin around here, but its been long enough to read the Grangerford/Shepherdson episode and I also make it thru the King and Duke episode. I'm just gettin into the part where the loafers are hangin around, chewin tobacco, when the original guy that put the arm on me outside comes rushin in and wants us five boys outside right away. I'm puttin the book away when he says to me,

"Come on, come on. Lets go, lets go," impatient, like I was holdin im up on purpose. I wanna say, "Fuck you, asshole," but I dont. I just get the book put away and get outa there.

We go back over to the set. Swede and Max are gone, and so is everybody else except the actors and crew on the set. The spectators musta got run off. We stand there for another hour watchin the Rascals go thru a scene. Finally, at around five oclock, someone says,

"Okay, lets break for dinner," and everybody starts wanderin off in different directions. The young girl comes over to the five of us and she's got a wad a bills as big as yer fist. She says theyre not gonna use us and peels off two ones for me and each of the four others, and then I head back over to the dressin room to get my bedroll and get the hell outa there. I got two bucks for my trouble, but what a wasted afternoon.

When I get back out onto Vine Street, I see James and Swede right away down at the corner a Sunset. Its already dark, and the Christmas decorations on the lamp posts and strung across the street are all lit up. My pals are hangin around by a newsstand. I walk down in their direction, and as I'm walkin, I all of a sudden start feelin real tired. I found out right there how sittin around doin' nothin can wear yuh out. I bet that's why I'm feelin so pooped. I'll take a good day's hustle over hangin around and loafin any day.

"Well, so much for bein a movie star," I say. "I wasted all that time, and I didnt even get into the goddamn movie."

"What happened?" Swede asks.

"Hell, you were there. You saw what we was doin'. The same as what you was doin'. We watched the Little Rascals go thru some scenes. That was it. And when it was over, they gave me two bucks and sent me on my way. Where'd you and Max go to?"

"They chased us off. Right after you went back to wherever you went, a guy came over and told us we had to take a hike. It was close to the time we was supposed to meet James anyway, so I just waited at the studio gate until he showed up, and now we been waitin these last couple hours for you to come out. Max went walkin off back to his hotel to meet his dad."

"Well, at least you got the money," James says. "That works out to a half buck an hour for just hanging around. Thatll be a part of your nest egg for getting started in California. I'm gonna help you out a little, too."

"Wha'da yuh mean yer gonna help me out? How yuh gonna do that?"

"Well, its like I told Swede earlier, I think we'll be splitting up tomorrow. Just let me finish," he says stoppin me from interruptin im. "I saw Lor-raine while you were being a movie star. She gave me twenty bucks, and she's gonna try to help me out some more. I'm gonna see her again tomorrow. It seems she's not doing too bad in the movies. She's making a good living. But the kicker is she's missed me just as much as I've missed her. She split up with the producer who brought her out here. Says theyre still good friends; she just couldnt live with im. And now that I've showed up, she says she wants to start it up again. We're getting together tomorrow to iron out a few things."

"Boy, a lot's happened in just a couple hours, aint it?" I say.

I'm kinda stunned by what's happenin here. I didnt think about when we'd be splittin up with James, and now here it is, and I dont know what to do.

"Look," says James, "since we've got plenty of dough, why dont we get us a nice hotel room with hot water, and then we'll go out and get us a first-class dinner. This is gonna be our last night together, so lets make it a good one."

That sounds good to me and Swede, so we start walkin back toward downtown Los Angeles on Sunset Boulevard. About two blocks up theres a place called the Hollywood Hawaiian Hotel, which is a little bungalow court like the one we stayed at in Acuña, Mexico. This one's a little cleaner and tidier than that one was, just like everything here is tidier and cleaner than in Mexico, but no different otherwise. We get a bungalow for fifty cents for the night. Its got hot and cold water, two beds and a fold out davenport. Checkin the rest a the court out, I figure its about half full. I only see two bungalows that dont look occupied. Now that's a big difference from Virgilio's place in Mexico. There were more vacant ones than occupied ones.

245

After we get settled into our room, we one at a time take showers. Nice feature. Theres plenty a hot water, and it sure feels good to stand under it for the ten or so minutes I spend there. It almost seems a shame to put these dirty clothes I been wearin back on over this clean body.

"Yuh know," I tell James while Swede's takin his shower, "we oughta see if we cant maybe find a clothes store somewhere around here and get us some new duds. The ones we got are lookin pretty ragged and dirty."

"That sounds like a good idea," James says. "I think we've got the dough to pay for them, and I did see some clothes stores up around Hollywood and Vine today when I was out looking for Lorraine."

Swede gets outa the shower and gets dressed, and we head out the door. Its only two blocks back to Vine and then two blocks up to Hollywood. As soon as we get onto Hollywood Boulevard, we see three clothes stores in the first block and theyre all still open. In the window a the first one we come to, theres a mannequin wearin khaki trousers and a flannel shirt. That's a pretty good lookin combination to me, so I walk right in and tell the clerk that I wanna try it on. He wants to see my money, and I don't blame him, before he takes my measurements. Then he finds the right sizes and sends me off to the dressin room. Once I get the clothes on, and I see that they fit okay, I roll my old clothes up in a bundle and go out to pay for the new ones. James gets some slacks, a shirt and a sport jacket that are a little more dressy than my outfit, and Swede gets khaki trousers, like me, and a navy-blue sweatshirt. James pays for the whole works with the twenty bucks Lorraine gave im. He gets seven dollars and some coins in change. We step out onto the street preenin like a bunch a damn peacocks in our new threads. At the corner a Hollywood and Vine, theres a city trash can, and that's where we dump our old clothes.

"Now," James says, "I think that cafe I saw earlier was down on Sunset a couple blocks past Vine. It looked like a really swell place to me. We might be able to get a good steak there. You boys interested in that?"

"Show us the way," Swede says.

We walk thru the front door to find a little restaurant, neat as a pin, with booths and tables with red checkered table cloths. Along the right wall is a counter with swivel stools anchored to the floor in front of it. The place is kinda busy right now, but I see two vacant booths in the back. The lady behind the cash register comes over to us with three menus in one hand. She leads us back to one a the vacant booths and sits us down. They got steak on the menu, New York cut and T-bone. All three of us get the New York cut with baked potatoes. James gets his cooked medium rare while me and Swede get ours done medium well. James uses the last four dollars and sixty-five cents a the twenty for the three steaks, and that includes the tip. I cant get over how much better this is than what I had back home. I bet if I wanted to, I could go back to that studio tomorrow and pick up another two bucks. No thanks. I couldnt take another day like today. Be-

247

sides I'm hopin we'll be on our way to Seal Beach to-morrow.

The steaks are so lean and tender that you can almost cut em with the edge a yer fork. I think this is the best meal I can ever remember havin in my life. Its damn sure the best I've had since Wiktor Sadlo moved in with Ma, and before that, too. I coulda had somethin this good a time or two when Pop was still around, but I sure dont remember it.

"The way I figure it," James says, "we'll meet Lorraine around ten oclock in front a Grauman's Chinese Theatre which is about a mile west of here. You boys interested in meeting Lorraine?"

"More'n just interested," I say. "I'm really lookin forward to it."

"Me too," says Swede.

When we finish dinner, James says we should go scout out this Grauman's Chinese Theatre by lookin it up tonight. Sounds like a plan to me, so after gettin directions from the waitress, we start walkin west on Sunset. This kinda reminds me of Beale Street and Bourbon Street only without the music, or the music is different anyway. Theres more neon here. It seemed like in those other places the music, played by trios, quartets and quintets, was comin outa every door you'd pass. Here you walk along for a while without hearin any music a-tall, and then you pass a good size night-club, and you can hear the sound of a seventeen-piece dance band floatin out the front door when it swings open to let someone in or out. This street's got the action just like those other two. Every once in a while a big Duesenberg or Packard passes by, and it must be movie stars drivin em. Who else could ever afford such nice cars?

We take a right at Highland Avenue, and right there on our left is Hollywood High School. Boy, what a nice lookin high school. I never seen a school in Minneapolis looked like this. Two blocks up is Hollywood Boulevard, and Grauman's Chinese Theatre is just off the corner. We walk over to it. In front is a big open courtyard area with a bunch a concrete squares, and some of em have hand and footprints in em with dates and movie star names.

"Well, this is it," James says. "She said she'd pull up in her car right out front here."

"Wow, yuh mean she's got her own car?" I say. "Sounds like she's got a pretty swell setup."

"Well, she isnt as big time as Clara Bow, but she's doing all right for what she does."

Its gettin close to ten oclock, so we start headin back to the Hollywood Hawaiian. Its Friday night and theres a lota people out and about. Cars are drivin up and down the streets, nice cars like Cadillacs, Buicks and Packards. The drivers're all actin like they expect to be recognized. So far I aint seen a one that I recognize from any movie I ever saw, and wha'da yuh know, theres the Buick we saw in Acuña and Del Rio. The old man's drivin and the girl's sittin next to im on the passenger side. I wonder if we'll see the bank robbers, too. The lamp posts along Hollywood, Vine and Sunset are all decked out with Christmas decorations. Theres a vacant lot on Sunset where a guy is sellin Christmas trees. As we pass, he turns out the lights he's got strung on the poles holdin up the chicken wire fence around his lot. He's goin inside a little tent he's got set up in one corner a the lot.

Its cold inside the bungalow when we get there, so we turn the radiator on and start gettin ready to hit the sack. I drop off as soon as I get under the covers, and I sleep straight thru. No dreams or wakin up in the middle a the night.

Twenty-eight

Ever since we been on the road, it seems we're always gettin up at the break a day. Course that aint a whole hell of a lot different from what I done at home. I guess I just carried the habit over when I struck out on my own and started ridin the rails. I used to try to be up and outa the house before the Polack got up just so I wouldnt have to mess with im. And it worked too, cuz I really never seen too much of im. When all's said and done, I guess I didnt see im seldom enough.

This mornin aint no different'n any a the other mornins in the last three weeks. We're all three up at dawn, which means we probly still have four hours before we meet Lorraine at the movie theater, but here we are wide awake and ready to go, and its barely light out a-tall. I crawl outa the sack and walk across the room to the window where I see Sunset Boulevard. Last night when we was walkin, there was a lot goin on. Cars were travelin up and down the streets, and people were out on the sidewalks. They was goin in and outa movie theaters, restaurants and drugstore soda fountains. The only thing out there now is a milk truck that's stopped in front of an apartment house down the street.

After we splash some water on our faces, we go across the street from the motel to the coffee shop and have breakfast: pancakes, eggs, sausage, orange juice and coffee for James, milk for me and Swede. We been lucky at gettin dough since we left home. Beginnin with the five bucks that floated into our hands in Milwaukee all the way to the deuce I picked up yesterday, we aint had nothin but good luck. The way we're eatin right now, you'd never know we was in the middle of a depression. By the time we finish breakfast and step out onto the street, the sun is up and Saturday mornin lazy is in the air. Theres people out, but nobody's in any rush to get anywhere. Its the weekend, and theyre off from work (those lucky enough to have jobs), so theyre just out hangin around or maybe casually on their way to the hardware store or someplace similar to get whatever it is they need to fix whatever's broken at home. The ones that aint got jobs are just hangin around, only now its on the weekend instead of a weekday.

We go back to our bungalow and get our stuff together. We still got a couple hours before its time to meet Lorraine, so we use the time to walk around and look Hollywood over in the daylight. We wanna get a high-up view of the city, so we go down to the next corner from our motel, Gower Street, and take a left and start walkin in the direction a the mountain. After we pass Hollywood Boulevard, we start climbin a fairly steep hill. Then the road starts to wind around up into a canyon. We come to a sign that says, "Dead End." There aint no road beyond the sign, but wheel ruts curve around the barricade and go along level for twenty feet or so into a small upward slopin valley that's sheltered on the north by the mountain and has a southern view a Hollywood and beyond. I bet this is pretty at night with the lights a the city out there. It looks like theres some kinda settlement or colony in the valley, and the people here look like theyre probly in show business. It dont look like no hobo jungle. Theres gypsy wagons, like the one in New Orleans where I got my Tarot cards read. Some a the people have tents set up with campfires burnin out front. Theres an old army ambulance from the war. Looks like a fella and his wife are livin in it. They got a canvas awning comin off the back, and theyre sittin at a table under it havin breakfast. Off to one side a couple jugglers are perfectin their act. This looks like the kinda place where Dillon mighta stayed. It looks safe and cozy, a good spot for an actor until he gets his break in the trade.

We turn around and go back to the roadblock where the "Dead End" sign is. The three of us sit up on the wooden cross bar a the barrier like the three monkeys that don't see no evil, hear no evil or speak no evil. We couldnt ask for a better view. Spread out right below us is Hollywood, and then beyond that is huge, flat open country with some hills off to the right. Then a long way off in the distance are some more hills, and right behind em it looks like the blue ocean, which bends up around on our right disappearin behind a mountain off in the west. It even looks like theres an island out there straight ahead and to our left. I aint sure. Could be just part a those hills off in the distance there by the ocean. But that is definitely the ocean, my first view of it. I wonder if I'm lookin at Seal Beach anywhere out there. Over on the left are the two tall buildings in downtown Los Angeles. Theres some other four-and five-story buildings all around em, but theyre not nearly as tall as the white one, and the black one aint even as tall as that. It sticks up so high cuz its on a hill, it looks like.

After stayin there for maybe a half hour, we start the trek down off the hill. At Hollywood Boulevard we take a right and start walkin toward the theater. What a street this is! I aint never seen so many movin picture shows all on one street. Must be two in every block, not even mentionin the jewelry stores, fancy clothes stores, and joints. Well, I guess joints aint the right word. These are real fancy nightclubs. I cant imagine how they do any business. Who's got that kinda dough anyway? Somebody must. We shoulda walked back to our motel down *this* street instead a Sunset. I bet more was goin on here than there. Hollywood and Vine seems to be the center a Hollywood. The tallest buildings around are right here on these four corners. The Taft Building and the Roosevelt Hotel. Now we're back where we was last night. It sure looks different in daylight. Things look real dirty in the bright sunlight. The place seemed flashy last night under the bright glow a neon that lit up the night.

We get to Grauman's Chinese Theatre at about a quarter to ten. Its still early, and there aint nobody out lookin at the hand and footprints a the stars. We're the only ones hangin around. I look down and I'm standin on the square with Tom Mix's hand and footprints. Right there in the same square are Tony's hoof prints. When I look up again, a lady in a brand-new Ford coupe pulls up to the curb. James walks out to meet her. He goes around to the driver's door and opens it for her. When they come around from the oth-

254

er side a the car, I'm lookin at a brunette that's probly one a the prettiest women I ever laid eyes on. You can tell she's a movie star. She's dressed to the nines, and she's just so soft-lookin and beautiful.

"Lorraine," James says, "may I present my traveling companions of the last month. Swede, Antoine, this is Lorraine."

"Pleased to meet yuh ma'am," we both say.

"Oh, the pleasure's all mine," she says. "James spent the better part of our two-hour visit yesterday telling me all about you two."

"Well, we sure been anxious to meet yuh," I say.

"Shall we go for a ride?" she says.

"Well," James says, "maybe we should find out how to get these boys to Seal Beach. What do you say, boys? Do you want to start looking for your aunt's place, Swede?"

"Well, I guess," Swede says. "I dont know how ready I am for it, but yeah, I guess we better start lookin for her. How about you, Antoine? You ready to split up with this guy?"

"I dont know if I'm ready or not, but I guess we gotta do it sometime."

"I think we can figure out how to get you to Seal Beach in no time," Lorraine says. "First we should go to the Pacific Electric Station downtown. I'm sure theres a Redcar that goes to Seal Beach, Long Beach at the very least, which would put you close enough to catch a local Long Beach streetcar that would take you to Seal Beach."

255

Jerome Arthur

We walk back out to her car, and she goes to the rumble seat and opens it. I climb up first; Swede's right behind me. This is a brand new thirty-one Model-A Ford, and it sure is a swell car. James and Lorraine get in up in front and we go chuggin off toward downtown Los Angeles. Its a clear, sunny day, but its a bit cold goin along at twenty-five miles an hour out in the open, but we're plenty warm cuz me and Swede kept our good jackets last night when we threw everything else away. We got our hands in our pockets so our faces are all that's cold, and it sure is fun ridin in this swell new car in Hollywood, California.

When we get back into downtown, I see James pointin at the tall white building, and then Lorraine takes a right at the next corner, which happens to be Broadway, and we're headin right for the place. She goes one block and takes a left on Temple. A half block down she pulls over and parks the car. We get out and walk the half block down to the tall white building which Lorraine has by now told us is the Los Angeles City Hall. James says we're gonna go to the top and take a look at the view.

We go right on Spring and cut across the street to the entrance at the top a some stony white steps. We walk thru some huge columns and cross a big open courtyard and into this brand-new looking building. Its Saturday so nobody's inside workin, only a couple security guards and an elevator operator. This is what they do on weekends, elevator tours to the top to see the view. Kinda like what I heard they do at the Empire State Building. So, we get on the elevator along with some out a town tourists, and a few minutes later we're

256

zipped up to the top where we go to an outside area with a high railin and we can see for miles around. You can walk all the way around, seein the snow capped mountains to the north and east and the ocean to the south and west with the black and gold Richfield building in the foreground just a few blocks away. That *was* an island I saw before. I see it more clear from this vantage point. Lorraine says its Catalina Island, about twenty-five miles off Long Beach. You can see the houses in the valleys and on the hills around us, and you can see open space way out beyond the city. We get back on the elevator and go down to the street.

"Well boys, I guess its about time to put you guys on a streetcar to Seal Beach, and then I'm going wherever this lady takes me," James says. "We're only a few blocks away from the Redcar depot."

"I never gave too much thought to when we'd be goin our separate ways," I say. "I guess I knew it had to come. Just a matter a time. I never really got ready for it."

"You gonna be okay?" Swede says to James. "I mean, is anyone lookin for yuh or what?"

"Doesnt seem to be," he says. "Lorraine says no one has ever come around to her. I think its going to be okay."

We all get into the car and Lorraine goes down two blocks to Main Street and takes a right. Then she drives another seven blocks thru the center a downtown. And what a nice downtown it is, too. We pull up next to a building with a sign that says, "Pacific Electric Depot." The four of us walk inside, and the first thing we do is look at the schedules and routes; there is a car that goes to Seal Beach (it actually goes all the way to Newport Beach accordin to this map), but it dont leave for another forty-five minutes. We just missed one five minutes ago. When we was comin down Main Street, I noticed a Western Union office a couple blocks back next to a beautiful, swanky-lookin hotel called the Rosslyn.

"Since we got almost an hour before our streetcar leaves," I say, "I wanna go to that Western Union and send a telegram back home."

"Well, I guess I'll give you your present now then," James says. He takes two ten-dollar bills outa his pocket and gives one to me and one to Swede. "These are from Lorraine and me to you two guys. Its not much, but its something to help you get started in your new life. And you keep all that money you've got stuffed in the lining of your coat. I dont want any of it."

"Gee, that's swell," I say. "Itll sure help if we dont get jobs right away."

"Here's where I'll be," James says handing me a piece a paper with an address on it. "Drop me a line when you get settled. Let me know where you are and how things are going for you. Maybe later we can get together and go do something."

At the Western Union I fill out the form to send Ma a telegram: "Dear Ma stop I'm alive and safe in Seal Beach, California stop With Swede stayin at his aunt's stop I'll write later stop Love, Antoine." It cost almost a half buck to send that telegram, but the clerk that sent it for me said it'd get there by this afternoon, so I guess its worth it. We walk around downtown for the last twenty minutes before our streetcar pulls out.

258

ANTOINE FAROT AND SWEDE

For bein so big, this town sure is pretty. People seem so friendly and casual, and the city is just plain beautiful. The weather's nice and everything seems so fresh and clean.

We get back to the depot five minutes before the streetcar is supposed to leave. We buy tokens from a clerk in a cage. This station is a lot like that booth we passed as we went into Juárez last Tuesday. We go stand on a platform near where our streetcar is supposed to leave from. It pulls in and shuts down, and the conductor and motorman get out and disappear into an inner office. While theyre doin' that, me and Swede are shakin hands with James and sayin goodbye to Lorraine. After a couple minutes, the conductor and motorman come out and board the car. Then me and Swede get on board, too, along with about a dozen other people. James and Lorraine are still standin on the platform when we sit down in our seats. The streetcar pulls out, and I see em turn and head outa the depot.

Twenty-nine

When the big red streetcar pulls outa the station, its on an elevated trestle that slants down and curves onto a city street. Looks like we're headin due south.

"I'm already missin James," I say. "How bout you?"

"Yeah, me too. He's a swell fella. We mighta been able to get this far without im, but you can bet yer ass it woulda been a lot harder, and we wouldnt be here yet. Without im we'd probly still be in New Orleans, or maybe not even that far."

"Makes me sad enough to cry," I say, chokin back my tears and starin out the window at the passin city.

Last time I remember feelin this sad was the first couple nights after we left home when I was so lonely and melancholy. We'll have to get in touch with im at the address he gave me after we get settled someplace and get jobs.

The conductor calls out the names a the stops as we roll along. Huntington Park looks like a nice little white picket fence neighborhood. Not two miles down the road, we go thru a place called Watts where the car stops and picks up seven colored people. Five are women, cleanin women they look like, and the other two are teenage boys. The teenagers get off a short distance down the road, Willoughbrook. The ladies continue on, gettin off at different stops further down the line. We go thru Compton, and we start movin away from the city. Up ahead are some rollin hills with a buncha wooden oil derricks on em. The conductor calls out "Dominguez Junction!" as the trolley pulls up to a platform. We roll south, and when we get to the hills, we bank a little to the left, skirtin em and runnin alongside a stream. Its amazin how this streetcar goes so far out into the country like this. For a short time here, I'm not seein any houses or streets or any other sign of civilization, except for the oil wells. Then we cross over a river and we're back into a town again. We curve left around a big hill with more oil derricks on it. We been curvin so much to the left that I think we must be goin almost due east by now. Looks like it accordin to where the sun is.

"Pacific Coast Highway, Long Beach, Signal Hill!" the conductor calls out.

On our right since we came around the hill, theres a sweepin view of a city that I'm guessin is Long Beach. It looks like its about as big as Minneapolis. Maybe not quite as big. That small mountain risin outa the blue ocean must be Catalina Island. Its such a clear day, we see details in the mountain. I still cant get over the palm trees; theyre all over the place down below us. The best word I can think of to describe em is "casual." The streetcar gets rollin again droppin down off the hill to leveler ground and into the populated neighborhoods of Long Beach. After our last stop in that town, we drop down into a low marshy spot with little waterways runnin out to the ocean.

"Naples Junction!" the conductor calls out, and we stop again. Ahead on our left are some more oil derricks on the side of a hill. As we pass em, we cross over a river right at its mouth where it runs into the ocean, and the conductor says,

"Seal Beach!"

So, this is it. We pull into a small seaside village. Most a the houses are small bungalows that look like rich people's vacation houses, like places up at the lake back home. The streetcar stops at the corner a Main Street and Electric Avenue. When the doors hiss open, a fresh ocean breeze hits me in the face. It smells briny and fishy. We step down and start walkin up Main Street toward the beach. Behind us we hear the streetcar pull out, clatterin off on its trip further on down the line. Main Street looks like somethin outa the wild west. The square wooden fronts on the shops and stores look like the storefronts of the town in that movie, Fightin Ranch, that I seen last year with Ken Maynard in it. The sidewalk is wood in some places and concrete in other places. One block has an old west weathered wood awning over the sidewalk. You almost expect someone to ride up on a horse and tie up to a hitchin rail. If you didnt have the smell, you'd never guess that you were only a couple blocks from the ocean. You'd think you was out on the prairie somewhere.

When we get to the beach, theres a couple bait shops at the foot of a pier. Waves are breakin thru the pier pilings and all along the beach. Swede takes the old crumpled envelope outa his bedroll. Its addressed to his mother and the return address is his aunt's.

262

ANTOINE FAROT AND SWEDE

"We only got a P.O. Box," Swede says, "so lets go back to that post office we just passed and ask where her house is gonna be."

We go back to the. P.O. A man inside the cage looks up when we go in. Swede goes up to im, and showin im the envelope, asks directions.

"What you do," the man says, "is go up one block to the beach. That's Ocean Avenue. You turn left and go one block to Tenth Street and take a right toward the beach. You go one block and you'll see a wooden walkway along the beach. It goes in front of the houses that are built right out there next to the sand. That's Seal Way. Now yer aunt lives at the other end of it, so yer gonna have to walk about a half mile till you come to her place. Its the last house at the end of that board walkway, right on the beach. Yuh cant miss it."

We thank im and start walkin. At the corner of Ocean and Main, theres a little fish restaurant named Nelson's. That makes Swede feel real welcome cuz that's his last name. Its just like when we was in New Orleans, and I saw that restaurant Antoine's, but that one was real swanky compared to this one. Before we turn onto Seal Way, I take a few steps out on the beach. Standing here with the beach and ocean on one side and the little shack-like houses backed by palm trees on the other, I feel like I'm standin in a tropical island paradise. We start walkin down the plank walkway toward the other end and Swede's aunt's house. What nifty little places these beach cottages along here are. Every one of em has a swell view a the ocean and a huge beach. We turn a small bend in the walk and now theres more vacant lots than theres houses. Up ahead

263

we see a woman hangin her laundry out on the clothes-line next to her house. She spots us as she's takin a dress outa her laundry basket. She straightens up and dont hang the dress up, but instead stands there starin at us with a look of disbelief. Swede raises his hand and gives her a real shy wave.

"My god, is that you, Helge?" she says and rushes over to us. "What're you doin' here?"

"Hi, Aunt Ingrid," Swede replies. "Its me all right. Me and Antoine here ran away from home. We wanna get work so we can stay."

"I already knew you ran away. I just got a letter from your mother day before yesterday," she says. "She said you'd been missing since Thanksgiving. She's awful worried. Thank God, yer safe. We'll just have to write a letter back to her as soon as possible. Well, come in the house."

Just as we start to follow her into the back yard, one a the crosses a the clothes line starts to give under the weight a her laundry hangin on it. Me and Swede run over and grab it, holdin it up while his aunt takes her clothes down. I guess me and Swede can get to fixin that right away. After she gets her clothes down, we let the cross down, layin it flat on the ground. Then we all go into the house.

The place is built up a little from beach level, so when yer at the back a the house, yuh gotta go up a few steps to get into the kitchen thru the back door. Right next to the back door in the service porch is her wringer washer next to a laundry sink. Goin into the kitchen, on our left is the kitchen sink and on our right is a counter with some cupboards underneath it. Its

264

open from the countertop to the ceilin, and lookin thru this open space from the kitchen is a dinin room and parlor combination. Straight ahead along the front wall are two windows and the front door all with views of the beach. Thru the front door across the whole front a the house is a covered porch with a couple chairs and a round table built from heavy wood. The house and porch are high up so you get a good view a the ocean and Catalina from the porch. You cant see em from down below on the board walkway cuz the beach kinda mounds up and blocks yer view. The parlor occupies the whole front part a the house. Two doors along the northwest wall go into the bathroom and bedroom. The bedroom is so small that it only has a double bed in it. She keeps her cedar wardrobe in the parlor in the space between the bedroom and bathroom doors. We take seats on the stools at the counter as she starts bustlin around the kitchen.

"You boys must be hungry," she says. "I have some lunch meat here. How bout if I make you sand-wiches?"

"I *am* kinda hungry," Swede says. "How about you, Antoine?"

"I wouldnt turn down a sandwich."

When she starts gettin the food ready, me and Swede go around the counter to see if we can help her with anything. She tells us to take the quart a milk outa the ice box and pour two glasses. While I'm doin' that, Swede's lookin out into the back yard thru a window over the kitchen sink.

"What's that?" he says pointin at a small building that looks like a garage on the alley that runs along the back a the property.

"That's where you boys are going to be staying. Its my garage. There is some stuff stored there, but it wont take us any time to rearrange things and get it ready for you to move in. Before we do that, we're going to have to sit down right away and write to your mother to let her know youre all right. How about you, Antoine. Should you be writing to your mother, too?"

"No ma'am," I say. "Just before we got on the streetcar to come down here, I sent her a telegram. She's probly already got it."

"Oh, very well. Here are your sandwiches then."

She sets em on the counter next to our glasses a milk. I wanna take my shoes and socks off and go out in the sand, so as soon as we finish eatin, while Swede and his aunt are writin a short note home to Swede's mom, I go out onto the beach and down to the surf. As warm as the weather is, that ocean is damn cold. The sand is cold under my bare feet. When I get back up to the house, they finished their letter. She wants to get it out before the afternoon mail pickup, so she's gonna take it up to the post office. Before she goes, she takes us out to the garage and shows us where to move the stuff that's stored in it. She says she'll help us when she gets back.

So, we start in on it, and after a couple minutes, I remember the clothes line, so I tell Swede I'll fix it, and he can keep cleanin out the garage. When I go out and look at it, I see I wouldnt be able to fix it proper without a post hole digger and an eight-foot piece a wood. Eyeballin the distance, I figure I can run the same ropes between the house and garage. All I need to do is unscrew the hooks from the cross bars, and screw em into the side a the house and garage.

The distance between the house and garage is actually less than between the two posts, so theres plenty a rope. I'm just finishing the job when aunt Ingrid comes back. Swede's just about got all the stored junk moved to one side a the garage. Aunt Ingrid hangs her clothes out, and then the three of us get busy sweepin and cleanin up the garage. One a the things Swede moved was a rug that was rolled up and stashed along a wall. After we get the concrete floor swept, we roll out the rug, and it almost covers. We can use some a the other stuff, too. Theres an army cot and a couple chairs. As the afternoon moves along, we manage to get a nice little room set up in the garage. For beds we got the army cot, and Aunt Ingrid also had a twin bed mattress one a her neighbors had stored in her garage. There aint no frame or box spring, so its right on the floor, but its plenty comfortable.

Its just before sunset by the time we finish gettin it set up, and we go into the house and start gettin ready for dinner. Me and Swede go to the front window and watch the sun sink behind the mountain off to our right. Then we get comfortable in the parlor and talk about our plan for gettin jobs while Aunt Ingrid fixes up some chili con carne and her homemade whole wheat bread. She tells us we should go to Long Beach to look for work.

"I'm sure its not much better out here than it was back in Minneapolis," she says, "but if there are going to be any jobs, theyll probably be in Long Beach, or Los Angeles, but that's a long way away from here. I guess the first thing to do is get the morning paper and see if anything's available."

The chili con carne tastes swell. Sure, is nice to have a home cooked meal again. Its so quiet and dark out there on the beach. When I finish my bowl of chili, I go out onto the porch and look at the black water where I see a small skiff movin silently away from a bigger boat a some kind. Its dark and I cant hardly make em out, but after strainin my eyes some, I'm sure its what I think it is.

"Hey, Swede," I call into the house. "What do you say we take a walk on the beach, see what's goin on out there."

He comes out the front door and after squintin into the darkness for a minute or so, he says,

"Whatre they doin'?"

"Dont know. Lets go take a look."

"Aunt Ingrid, me and Antoine're gonna go out and have a look at the beach. We'll be right out here in front."

"Okay," she says from the kitchen.

We go out the front door, across the porch, down the steps and onto the beach. We cut across the beach toward a small inlet that's sheltered from the surf. The dinghy has gone in there. A hundred feet or so to the left is an old Model-T pickup truck backed up to the beach where a dirt road comes to a dead end. Two fellas are standin by next to a dropped down tailgate. Theres only one man on the skiff and he has now jumped off and is pullin it up in the sand. The two next to the pickup truck scurry across the sand to help im. The only cover out here is the darkness, and there aint much a that cuz the moon's almost full, so we cant get too close to see what theyre doin', but theyre so busy doin' it that we get to within about thirty feet of em and they still dont notice us. Then a cloud covers the moon, hiding us for a minute or two.

"Is this the hundred proof stuff," one a the men from the truck says to the one from the skiff.

"You got it. Top quality scotch and bourbon. You got the cash?" the other says.

"You bet," said the first. "Its in the truck. Lets each take a case a this stuff, and you can get it before we finish the rest a the load."

"Bootleggers, or smugglers," I tell Swede as we walk out toward the surf. "You can see a bigger boat out past the waves."

"Yeah, I see it," he says.

We cut back across the sand toward the house. Aunt Ingrid's washin dishes in the dim kitchen light. We tell her what we saw, and she says it goes on all the time here.

"I dont know why they dont just do away with prohibition," she says. "It seems that all its doin' is makin crooks out of a lota people just because they like to have a drink once in a while. Prohibition never stopped anybody from drinkin."

"I know what yuh mean," I say. "My pop never had a problem gettin it."

"Mine neither," says Swede.

"And someone like *him* should be the last person to get his hands on it," Aunt Ingrid says. "I dont want to say anything against your father, Helge, but I dont think he should drink."

"I cant disagree with that," Swede says. "Why do yuh think I'm here with you right now, and not back home with him?"

We sit and talk like that till about ten oclock. Clouds are gatherin outside, blockin out the moon and stars. By the time we're ready to turn in for the night, its sprinklin. When me and Swede get into the garage, its a steady downpour, and it keeps up off and on all night long.

270

Thirty

After I get into bed, my nipples start gettin real hard and theyre hurtin again. They been doin' this off and on for a while. The last time it happened was a couple three weeks ago when I left home. It went away when we was at Oscar's farm, and now is the first its happened since then. I dont know what's causin it, but I wish it would quit. Right now, its keepin me awake, but soon enough, just from plain tiredness, I do drop off to sleep.

I have this dream where I'm over at Columbia Park out in north east Minneapolis, and I'm with Kathleen Knight, one a the girls from school. We're off in the trees, and all of a sudden she grabs me and starts kissin me and pullin my clothes off. I wake up to the sudden spurt a jizz in my boxer shorts. It feels good when it happens, but its damn uncomfortable havin a clammy wet spot in my shorts stickin to my leg. As I run my hand over my nipples, I can feel that theyre not hard anymore and they quit hurtin. In minutes I'm asleep again.

It rains off and on thru the night, a couple times pretty hard. This garage aint airtight or insulated in any way, and theres winds with the rain, so we're not too awful warm in here. Good thing we got those extra blankets in Arizona. Swede's aunt Ingrid had blankets for us so now we each got three heavy blankets, and its workin pretty good. This new Indian blanket is heaviest of all; I got it over Ingrid's blanket, and my wool army blanket is on top a everything. Its kinda dirty after all the miles its traveled. And we're damn lucky that Aunt Ingrid had this rug. It takes a lota the chill outa the cold concrete floor. One thing for sure, its absolutely dry in here. The roof dont leak one bit, but cuz theres no ceilin or overhead insulation, the rain really drums loud above us. Reminds me of my loft back at Oscar's farm, but that was warmer'n this.

When mornin rolls around, the rains comin down real hard. At the breakfast table Ingrid tells us its a welcome sight. She says they had a dry year last year, and theyre hopin to make up for it this year, so if they could get some more storms like this one, things'd be okay. I dont see any farm land anywhere around that looks like it needs rain, but I'm sure there must be some somewhere nearby that could use it. The wet beach looks weird, all raindrop-riddled and dappled. Out past the beach, you cant tell where the iron gray ocean (and to think it was so blue just yesterday) stops and where the dark clouds start. It all runs together. Dark. Tomorrow's the shortest day a the year.

"I guess we got rained outa lookin for jobs today," I say. "It'd be kinda hard to look for work in weather like this. Sunday's no day for it anyway."

"I suppose youre right," Aunt Ingrid says. "You could go to the grocery store on Main Street and get some newspapers and see what's in the want-ads."

"That sounds like a good plan," Swede says, gettin his two cents worth in.

We have some breakfast and then we just laze around waitin for the rain to let up. It never does stop completely today, but at one point it turns into a mist. That's our chance to go, so we take it. Ingrid gives us her umbrella and we go out the door. We dont get too far before it starts comin down again, so we hurry along and get to Main Street before we get too soaked. Most a the sidewalk on Main Street is covered, and once we get there, we manage to stay out of it pretty good. The newspaper racks at the store have a Long Beach Press-Telegram, a Santa Ana Register and three Los Angeles papers. The Long Beach and Santa Ana papers are only a penny, and the others are two cents each, so we just go ahead and grab all of em. We walk back to Ingrid's, and when we get to the end a the cover on Main Street, we stop and look at the ads and wait to see if the rain'll let up.

The Long Beach paper is lookin for someone to do a paper route in Seal Beach. Now that might be somethin for starters. I know it probly dont pay much money, but it'd be somethin. Least I've done it before. I had a Tribune route when I was twelve. I'd need to get a bike, but then maybe not. I bet there aint two hundred houses in the whole village, probly no more'n fifty papers, and its all flat, not a hill anywhere in town. Yuh gotta go a mile past Pacific Coast Highway before you come to a hill, and there aint no houses out there, just oil derricks. I could do a flat route like that on foot. There aint much else in the paper. A restaurant on Ocean Boulevard in Long Beach needs a dishwasher. Swede shows me a couple in the Los Angeles papers that are lookin for busboys in a brand-new downtown cafeteria just opened. Course if we went to work up there, we'd have to move there so we could live close to work.

Both agreein we dont have to find somethin right this minute, we start our hike thru the rain back along the beach to Ingrid's house. By the time we get there, we're soaked from the waist down, so we take our wet clothes off, hang em over chairs near the radiator and wrap dry towels around our waists till our trousers get dry.

We spend most a the day hangin around inside watchin the rain on the beach. At one oclock Ingrid grabs her umbrella and goes out to go to work at a big fancy house up at the other end a town on Ocean Avenue. She does house cleanin there on Mondays, Wednesdays and Fridays. She's goin to-day to help out at a Christmas party theyre havin. The people are a middle age couple that are real rich. He made a fortune in oil in the twenties and managed to hang onto it after Wall Street went haywire. Ingrid says every once in a while they have these Sunday afternoon affairs where a bunch of other rich people come over for cocktails and or derves, and he hires waitresses with shiny black skirts and white aprons to pass out refreshments. Ingrid works in the kitchen. She's the housekeeper when it aint a party. She says she gets a real good wage, which helps her make ends meet.

Me and Swede just hang around all afternoon starin out at the beach and waitin for the rain to let up. It does for a short time, and we chance a walk on the beach. We go all the way out to the high tide line and walk straight up the windy beach toward Long Beach. The clouds have lifted enough so you can see the Long

274

ANTOINE FAROT AND SWEDE

Beach skyline curvin to the left and is it beautiful against the stormy sky and that big mountain behind it. Storm seas and big surf complete the picture. Its all real dramatic lookin. As we walk along the beach, sand crabs make little air holes in the sandy ebb tide. We walk under the pier, and a little ways beyond it, we start seein these real fancy houses built up on the bluff on Ocean Avenue. Theres only a few of em, and each one has an ocean view from two levels a decks and picture windows. You couldnt ask for a bigger yard; the beach is right out the front door and across the street. Theres a party goin on in the last house before you come to the river mouth. That must be where Ingrid is. Some a the people are out on the deck takin advantage a the break in the storm and to look at the rainbow off to the northwest over Long Beach.

We turn around and head back home. When we get back to where we came out on the beach, we keep walkin on the shoreline until it bends back to the little inlet where those bootleggers were unloading their hooch last night. Its where the road next to the Redcar tracks ends and the tracks go across a bridge next to the highway south to Huntington Beach and Newport Beach. About another half block up, theres a small dock goin off the beach and into the water, and theres a little dirt road that comes off the street so people that wanna go fishin off the dock can drive their cars in and park close to it. The sign posted next the road where the pavement stops and the dirt starts says, "Anaheim Landing." This looks like it'd be a real keen swimmin hole. I guess we'll find out next summer. Just when we turn around to go back to Aunt Ingrid's

275

house, the rain starts up again. We get back inside, and then its like somebody opened up the sky. It's a cloud-burst.

The sky gets darker when afternoon changes to evenin. Ingrid arrives at sunset, and she did so well on that job that she wants to take us out to dinner. She says she'll take us to Nelson's, the little fish restaurant up on Main and Ocean, which sounds good to me cuz itll be the first time I'll have ocean fish from California. The rain starts to ease off to a drizzle at around six oclock, so with Swede carryin the umbrella and me and Ingrid hangin on each of his arms, we walk up to the restaurant without gettin very wet a-tall.

When we sit down at a table, we start talkin about what we're gonna do tomorrow. Earlier me and Swede talked about maybe takin the streetcar into Long Beach and lookin around down there for jobs. We tell Ingrid about it, and she says we can take the streetcar that stops at Main and Ocean straight down Ocean into downtown Long Beach. We're all lookin forward to it bein a big day.

"And when you get back, whatever time it is, we can go get a Christmas tree from that lot on the corner of the highway and Main Street," Ingrid says. "Would you boys be wanting a Christmas tree? I really hadn't been planning on getting one this year, but since you boys showed up, I've been thinking more and more about doing it."

"Yeah, I want one," says Swede. "I'll even help yuh decorate it. Its been a long, lonely trip out here, and I need some Christmas spirit. Maybe a tree'll give us some."

276

ANTOINE FAROT AND SWEDE

I do believe he's on the verge of cryin. I didnt realize he was so lonesome and homesick. Without no snow on the ground, I nearly forgot its even Christmas a-tall. She can either get a tree or not. It dont matter to me one way or the other.

We get a big order a fish and chips, and all three of us share from it. Its good. Ocean fish, like snapper, sure is different than walleye and northern pike, what I'm used to. When we finish eatin and step back out onto Main Street, the rain has stopped completely, but theres no moon or stars in the sky cuz its so cloudy. The wet street shines like glass reflectin the glow a the street lamps.

Back at the house we sit around listenin to the radio. We listen to a couple serials, and while theyre goin, Ingrid clears away an area in the front window for the Christmas tree. After movin a table with a lamp and a chair over into a corner, she joins us in listenin to the radio. When the shows are over, she turns the radio off, and we sit for a few minutes watchin the cloudy night sky clear up. Moon and stars are startin to show their faces from behind the clouds.

At nine oclock, me and Swede go out to our garage room and hit the sack. Swede goes right to sleep; I read Huckleberry Finn in bed for about five minutes, and then I fall asleep, too.

Thirty-one

We're two days into winter and two days till Christmas. Yesterday mornin me and Swede caught the trolley into Long Beach. When we got to the restaurant on Ocean Boulevard that wanted a dishwasher, there was at least fifteen fellas lined up for the job. We didnt even bother to get in line. Instead we got off Ocean and went up Locust Avenue where there was a couple buildings under construction. Not really expectin anything from it, we took the odd chance of askin a guy that looked like the foreman if he had any work for us. Well, believe it or not, he had somethin, but he only needed one guy, not two, and he needed a big guy. The guy he had for laborer just up and walked off the job not fifteen minutes before we got there, so he took on Swede, and it looks like he's gonna be workin there for a while, until they finish the building, couple months maybe, or longer.

I left Swede on the job, and then I stuck around town for a couple hours randomly goin in the front doors a different places askin for work. I found out real quick that there just aint no work available for me, at least not here, not now. So, I went back over to the construction site where Swede was, and I told im I was headin back to Seal Beach and I'd see im when he got back home. Before I got on the streetcar, I found the newspaper office and walked over there. After fifteen minutes of shufflin from one office to another, I ended up in the circulation office where I got the job of deliverin forty-five afternoon Press-Telegrams to the scattered houses around the little town a Seal Beach. They gave me a canvas bag with pouches front and back and a hole to put my head thru dead-center in the flat part a the canvas. "Long Beach Press-Telegram" was stenciled on the pouches. I gave em Ingrid's address, and they told me I'd be startin that afternoon. My bundle would be delivered at about one-thirty. The job paid ten-fifty a month, and I figured it couldnt take me more'n an hour a day to fold the papers and deliver em on foot. Compared to the job Swede got, it aint much, but its somethin. I'd sure as hell have plenty a spare time to do somethin else. I got ideas of hangin around on the beach when the weather got warmer. Course I'd still look for more work.

I leave the newspaper office and go to Ocean Boulevard to get the streetcar back to Seal Beach. I aint back at Ingrid's more'n forty-five minutes when a man shows up in the alley in a twenty-six Dodge businessman's coupe with a bundle a newspapers and a street map a Seal Beach. He shows me on the map, makin X's where I should deliver the papers, how I should cover the route, by makin a rough circle startin at Ingrid's house goin south, followin the shoreline until I come to the road next to the streetcar tracks. Then I'm supposed to take that straight up to the San Gabriel River and zigzag onto the cross streets makin deliveries. Then I come straight back down Ocean makin deliveries there and on the side streets until I get back to Ingrid's house. He goes thru it with me again to make sure I'm gonna do it right. He drives off with his last

279

couple bundles in the big trunk, and I start foldin my papers. It takes me a good hour and a quarter to do the route, only cuz I aint familiar with the streets and narrow alleyways where some a my customers houses are. I think I can cut the time back to fifty minutes when I get used to it. I know eventually I'll get it down to forty or forty-five minutes. I've already got the route down far as knowin the houses where I gotta throw papers, and aint gonna be long before I'm gonna be bored with it. If I can find me an old bike somewhere, that'd speed it up some.

I deliver to a couple a the businesses on Main Street, like the bait shops up by the pier and Nelson's fish restaurant where we ate last night. Theres also a small print shop and a real estate office on my route. I'll get to know the people that run these places, and I figure maybe if a job comes up, I could get it, but I wouldnt make book on my chances there, cuz there aint a real lot happenin in this sleepy little beach town. These folks are barely makin enough to support themselves. There aint no way they can even think about takin on hired help.

When Swede got back home Monday night, he was dog tired, but feelin good from workin hard and makin some dough to boot. After he got cleaned up and the three of us sat down to eat, he told us what he did all day. Mostly he was movin lumber around and helpin the carpenters, but he was also pickin up the scraps and dumpin em into a big trash bin. He says he did some diggin, too.

After dinner, we walk over to the Christmas tree lot at the highway and Main Street. Ingrid picks

out a five-foot-tall tree thatll fit real nice in the spot she
cleared in her parlor. I keep callin it that, but I'm findin
out that in California they call it the livin room. Goin
back home Swede takes the bottom and I grab it a couple feet down from the top. He leads the way, and we
carry it back to the house. We stand it up in the spot
Ingrid had cleared the night before and it fits perfect.
Over the next hour and a half Ingrid and Swede trim
away at it with strings of electric lights, ornamental
hangin balls and tinsel icicles. I stay outa their way by
gettin comfortable on the davenport and readin my
book. When the tree's decorated, we all go to bed.
Swede's gotta make sure he gets up early enough to
catch the streetcar into Long Beach.

I spent most a this mornin doin' nothin. I
walked around town a couple times. At one point I
walked straight out Ocean Avenue and crossed the
bridge over into Long Beach, a place called Belmont
Peninsula and Belmont Shore. The Peninsula is a kinda
wind blown little sand spit that looks like it'd be under
water if one big wave hit its shores. About a half mile
beyond the Peninsula is Belmont Shore, and now that's
a cute little beach town with a bustlin business street,
Second Street.

I looked around there for a while and decided
I'd come back again later and maybe look for work.
Theres little cottages with businesses in em. Theres a
couple barber shops, some real estate offices, a drugstore with a soda fountain, restaurants and a couple
corner groceries. They even got a picture show. I got a
good look at all these places, and then I headed down
Ocean Boulevard and crossed the bridge back into Seal

281

Beach. Goin back to Seal Beach from Belmont Shore is like goin to the other side a the tracks. That's how different the two towns are. I go straight down Ocean Avenue, and when I get to the pier, I go right and walk out to the end. There are quite a few people, men and women, fishin off the sides. I go out to the end and stare out at the horizon and think about Ma and Sis and Minneapolis. Then I go back in, and when I get back home, my papers are there, so I go in and get somethin to eat and then I go do my route.

When I finish it and get back home, Swedes already there. They ran outa stuff for im to do so they sent im home early. It was okay with him cuz he was still tired from the day before. I was pretty tired myself from all the walkin around I did, so we just relaxed and listened to the radio for a while, and then I started readin some more from Huck Finn. We hit the sack around ten oclock.

*   *   *

This mornin Swede was on his way back to work on schedule. I go down to the print shop on Main Street as soon as he opens. The printers name is Charlie, and he's the last delivery on my route. I stopped after I delivered his paper and talked to im a couple times while he was runnin the press. I watched im work, and it looks like fun. I'd like to maybe learn how to run a press myself. He could maybe teach me how. I go down there this mornin to watch im.

"I'm real interested in learnin this here trade from yuh. I need a job real bad too," I say.

282

ANTOINE FAROT AND SWEDE

"You and everbody else in this country, son. Tell yuh what. I'll think about it. Don't get yer hopes up. Kinda slow cuz a this damn depression. I'll let yuh know when yuh bring my paper this afternoon."

At eleven oclock, after watchin im finish a job, I walk up to the post office to pick up the mail. Theres three letters and one bill. One a the letters is addressed to me care of Ingrid Johnson. I recognize my Sis's handwritin on the envelope. I walk up to the pier and sit down on a bench overlookin the beach. I open the letter and read:

Dear Antoine,

As regards your recent telegram to your mother, I'm sorry to inform you that she never had a chance to read it, having passed away last Tuesday afternoon. The doctor said she died of complications from pneumonia. She took sick not two days after you left the house that dreadful night you almost killed poor Wiktor, and she just never got better. She suffered from high fever and chills and couldn't eat any food to speak of. I don't know what else to say about it. She's gone, and I miss her. You don't have to trouble yourself by coming home. She was buried on Saturday, so you missed seeing her and she you. I hope you're happy with your new life in California.

Your sister,

Megan

All of a sudden my goddamn heart is in my stomach. Goddamn it! Ma's dead! Shit! I wanna scream. If I could just scream, maybe I'd feel better,

283

but I doubt it. Megan makes it sound like its my goddamn fault, like what I done to Wiktor is what killed
her. I wonder if she's right. Now my heart's gone to
my throat, and I'm bawling like a baby. Oh, Ma, I'm
sorry, if I'm the one that caused you to die. I didnt
mean to. It wasnt supposed to be you; it was supposed
to be the Polack.

I'm sittin here starin out at the beach, the pier
and the ocean, not seein none of it. I dont know how
much time has gone by, but I know it must be gettin
close to time to deliver my papers, so I stir myself and
go draggin off to Ingrid's house and start foldin newspapers. I deliver to the businesses on Main Street last,
and when I make the delivery at Seal Beach Print
Shop, Charlie tells me he's been thinkin about what we
was talkin about this mornin, and he's decided to put
me to work as a feeder and oilin the press and sweepin
the floor and generally keepin the shop tidy. He's gonna pay me fifty cents a day for three hours work in the
mornin Monday thru Friday. And itll be cash under the
table so I dont have to worry about Uncle Sam. That's
a little more'n what I make for the hour I spend doin'
the route. Its a small wage, but I'll be learnin a trade,
and thatll make up for the low pay. I'm thankful he's
payin me anything. This is a start. Maybe he'll teach
me how to run the press, too. Its a good opportunity
and I know its gonna work out, but right now it seems
pretty hollow next to the news about Ma. I might as
well get started with it, tho, cuz I know I'm not goin
back home. I cant see Ma, and I dont wanna see Wiktor
and Megan cuz theyll only make me feel like it was my
fault that Ma died. I tell Charlie I can start any time, so

ANTOINE FAROT AND SWEDE

I just hang around with im for the rest a the afternoon,
and I start learnin right away.

The End

1989-2019

About the Author

Jerome Arthur grew up in Los Angeles, California. He lived on the beach in Belmont Shore, a neighborhood in Long Beach, California, for nine years in the 1960s. He and his wife Janet moved to Santa Cruz, California in 1969. These three cities are the settings for his ten novels.